FREE DVD FREE FREE DVD

Essential Test Tips DVD from Trivium Test Prep

Dear Customer,

Thank you for purchasing from Trivium Test Prep! We're honored to help you prepare for your Certified Corrections Officer Exam.

To show our appreciation, we're offering a **FREE** *Certified Corrections Officer Exam Essential Test Tips* **DVD** by Trivium Test Prep. Our DVD includes 35 test preparation strategies that will make you successful on the Certified Corrections Officer Exam. All we ask is that you email us your feedback and describe your experience with our product. Amazing, awful, or just so-so: we want to hear what you have to say!

To receive your **FREE** *Certified Corrections Officer Exam Essential Test Tips* **DVD**, please email us at 5star@triviumtestprep.com. Include "Free 5 Star" in the subject line and the following information in your email:

1. The title of the product you purchased.
2. Your rating from 1 – 5 (with 5 being the best).
3. Your feedback about the product, including how our materials helped you meet your goals and ways in which we can improve our products.
4. Your full name and shipping address so we can send your **FREE** *Certified Corrections Officer Exam Essential Test Tips* **DVD**.

If you have any questions or concerns please feel free to contact us directly at 5star@ triviumtestprep.com. Thank you!

- Trivium Test Prep Team

* Please note that the free DVD is <u>not included</u> with this book. To receive the free DVD, please follow the instructions above.

Table of Contents

Part I: The CCO Examination

CCO Overview

Congratulations for choosing to train as a corrections officer within the United States criminal justice system. In so doing, you have taken steps ahead in a career that not only advances your personal goals, but also demonstrates your commitment to serve the community and the nation.

At this point, your primary objective is to become a certified corrections officer (CCO), who wields an advanced knowledge of the corrections practice and operations. You are to achieve this by sitting out the standardized testing, and then earning the passing grade in the overall credentialing process, to prove that you deserve the professional certification.

Not everyone who has had the training and experience as a corrections officer becomes a bona fide, true-blooded CCO. Many who are eligible—a lot of whom are seasoned corrections officers—do not pass the exam. This is simply because of their attitude toward test-taking itself. Where some of them tend to be overconfident that they under-prepare for the exam or get careless with their answers, others are suddenly gripped by fear upon seeing confusing questions.

This CCO study guide is formulated to improve your performance during the test, to help you prepare in body, mind, and spirit for the professional certification. The process involves planning your strategy, from reviewing to test-taking, and gaining mastery of the key aspects in the field of corrections.

Remember that the CCO exam is not to be taken for granted; this is the crucial test of your mettle as a corrections officer. However, don't psych yourself out - as long as you know how to approach and conquer the challenge, you will pass with flying colors.

Building a Strategy

The primary objective of Part I is to help you build a study and test-taking strategy that will prepare you for this crucial step in your career. The key points show how to prepare your mind, body, and spirit, in order for you to absorb as much essential information as you can. Part I also reminds you of the "dos and don'ts" during the application and post-test periods.

A Step toward Professionalism

The Certified Corrections Officer (CCO) examination measures a candidate's knowledge of the corrections practice and operations acquired through training and experience.

The method that the CCO examination uses is standardized nationwide, and applies to work environments at the federal, state, and local levels. The design and development of the CCO examination is guided by experts in the field of corrections, including former and current public officials, persons of the academe, and research specialists.

Passing the examination grants the candidate his or her professional certification, which is proof of both capability and potential to assume higher responsibilities in the service. The result of the CCO examination is sent directly to the candidate, and cannot be furnished to anyone else without the candidate's written consent.

It is important to note that a professional certification is revocable under circumstances like a criminal conviction, administrative sanction for disciplinary reasons, or other examples that demonstrate a CCO's serious disregard for professionalism, ethics, and respect for the institutions and communities they are sworn to serve.

Eligibility

Any individual who has received training and/or experience as a corrections officer (adult corrections or juvenile justice) is eligible to take the CCO examination. An academic prerequisite is a high school or a general educational diploma, although federal candidates need to have at least an associate degree. Copies of the transcript are required in most cases.

Application Process

The application process is in itself a test of abilities, including an individual's compliance with rules and regulations. Incomplete or incorrect responses to items in the application packet may result in ineligibility to take the CCO examination for the testing cycle.

Application requirements typically consist of the following:

- Application Form
- Supporting Documents, as enumerated in the packet
- Payment of the Examination Fee

As a reminder, forms must be properly filled out, signed, and submitted according to instructions found in the application packet. Otherwise, the application will not be processed and the applicants' resources (non-refundable payments, other expenses incurred, effort, and time) will have been wasted.

Qualified test-takers will receive their permits or admission slips via post, courier, or e-mail. No walk-ins will be allowed during the test.

Preparation

The examination assumes that all CCO candidates have chosen the self-study programs and study guides that they think are ideal for helping them pass the test. Depending on their individual schedules and capacities, the entire process can take weeks or months to finish. What is important is being fully refreshed on the lessons learned from training and experience within the corrections profession.

Using This Study Guide

Getting a thorough grasp of essential terms and key concepts is important. The following are basic methods to help you internalize ideas from this study guide and other related material:

- Skim through the entire guide first without copying or highlighting
- Review the guide again this time contemplating terms and concepts
- Highlight the important parts ONLY after reading each section
- Clarify the vague parts by reading related material
- Look up unfamiliar words in the dictionary
- Read portions out loud: Hear your voice, listen to yourself
- Take notes

This is important: Do not surf the Web during your study hour! doing this will break your concentration. List unfamiliar phrases and clarify with veritable Internet sources after you are finished studying.

Taking Notes

Pairing reading with writing will optimize the process. Doing this will not only let you organize the terms and concepts reviewed; it will also allow you to summarize and express them in your own words.

Although you can treat the study-guide printout as a textbook/workbook, it is highly recommended that you keep a separate physical (not digital) spiral notebook where you can write down ideas relevant to the topics. Legal pads will not work as effectively because the leaves can be easily ripped off, increasing the odds of losing your precious notes.

Additionally, write down key words and phrases on an index card. Arrange the stack alphabetically and keep it in a box. Bring the entire set to work so you can review them during your break.

The following are supplies that will help with your studies:

- Physical notebook (not a pad of paper)
- Set of differently colored writing pens and highlighters
- Sticky tabs to mark pages
- Stack of index cards, organized in a box.

Your Environment

At home, find a quiet and properly lit corner away from your bed, TV, or whatever tends to distract you. De-clutter the space and use it as your review hub, a place where you can place all your materials and concentrate. If possible, limit the furniture and furnishings to a desk and a chair with a backrest that lets you sit up straight. Be sure that the overhead light or portable lamp does not strain your eyes with inadequate illumination or too much glare.

Your Schedule

A total of ten hours of focused review per week is better than forty hours of staring blankly at the study guide and absorbing nothing. Build "quality time" around your top priorities and routines in such a way that you are not worrying about tasks, chores, and deadlines while you are studying. Anxiety will block your thoughts and weaken your grasp of the subject material.

Do not read continuously for more than an hour. Rise from your seat, take a five- to ten-minute break and freshen up, then return to your desk.

Do not spend too much effort in searching for comprehensive test-taking tips and tricks, scrounging for unconventional secrets to passing the test, and memorizing things like how to perfect guesswork. There are no shortcuts. Devote your time to broadening and deepening your knowledge instead; act like any true-blooded, ethical corrections officer who understands the profession, and who deserves the certification!

The Examination

The CCO examination tests you for these abilities:

- Reading and understanding information
- Explaining and applying information
- Gathering data, facts, and other information
- Working with names, numbers, and symbols
- Organizing information and records
- Writing reports

During your review and preparation, aspects to consider in your study include conditioning the body, the mind, and the spirit to avoid untoward incidents that could prevent candidates from taking the test, or from answering correctly.

Physical

Proper nutrition, exercise, and hygiene will keep candidates fit enough to retain terms and concepts in their memory. A healthy and clean body will also minimize distractions like upset stomach, headache, or skin irritation.

Psychological

Mental calisthenics and meditation will balance the emotions, and enable a better absorption of ideas and a more critical analysis of situations.

Morale

Rest and recreation lift the spirits, and ensure that the body and the mind are synchronized enough to function effectively while studying (as well as during the test.) Time management is also important in ensuring readiness; cramming will only deplete your morale and erode your confidence.

The Eve of the Examination

On the day before the test, candidates are advised to eat a proper meal, take a shower, relax, and get eight hours of sleep. Among the benefits of doing these tasks in succession is avoiding the feeling of exhaustion, hunger, drowsiness, and panic while taking the test.

Spend this day preparing the items in the test-taking checklist provided by the CCO examination administrator. The checklist includes the admission slip or test permit, pencils, and such articles as driver's license, employment ID, and copies of supporting documents. Without these items, you will not be allowed to take the test. Don't forget to set your clothes out the night previously - clothes must be comfortable and should comply with the guidelines for CCO examination-takers.

The Examination Proper

The CCO examination takes place on the date stated in the admission slip. The test is proctored, and any applicant caught cheating in the room or in the premises will be disqualified from proceeding with the test. In some cases, a dishonest applicant will be rendered ineligible to take the test within the next five (5) years. Cheating is not limited to copying answers from other test-takers or referring to notes; it can also mean taking the test in someone else's place or engaging in "leakage."

Unless otherwise stated in the application guidelines and examination procedures, no candidate is allowed to bring any kind of food and beverage inside the testing room. There are also restrictions for clothing: Sweaters or jackets are permissible, but headwear (hat, cap, bonnet, other) is not. Watches are allowed, except those with calculators and functions that aid in answering questions.

Under no circumstances are candidates allowed to bring weapons and devices (calculators, laptops, tablets, cellular phones, cameras), to smoke, to record the examination proceedings, or to refer to study guides or notes.

No late-comers will be admitted. Those who have been through emergency situations at the time of the examination may be considered for the next testing period, provided they inform the administrators and furnish proof of their condition. However, they will still be prohibited from taking the test on the day they are tardy.

Exam Content

The CCO examination contains multiple-choice questions (MCQs) that test the candidates' knowledge and practical application of basic skills, as well as their understanding of important aspects in the field of corrections.

Although the questions are categorized, the test does not need to be answered in a numerical sequence. Candidates may skip and answer the easier MCQs first, then go back to the items that require more time to contemplate and analyze.

Duration

Depending on the administrators, the CCO examination may take as long as four hours. Candidates are usually expected to arrive one hour before the examination.

Reminders When Taking the Examination

Weeks upon weeks of dedicated studying can go to waste if you are not alert during the test. As mentioned earlier, careless responses and confused reactions to the questions are the most common culprits that pull down the overall score.

Taking Things One at a Time

Although it is not a definitive test of intelligence and emotional quotients, the CCO examination measures the candidate's reactions and approaches toward practical circumstances and possible events. The proper application of elementary math and language skills is therefore necessary.

Read and understand the question first before looking at the choices. If you already had an answer in mind, just pick it out from the choices and do not dwell on the item anymore. This gains you more time in contemplating the trickier questions.

Questions require answers that are either based on facts and absolute information, such as legal terms and concepts, or based on analysis of hypothetical situations.

Skip Ahead

If the choices leave you stumped, mark the item and return to it after answering the less challenging questions. If you still have no idea what to put when you have gone back to it, trust your instinct and make a guess.

Distracters (Trick Questions)

Designed to confuse and trap you, "distracters," also known as trick questions, may appear on the examination. These could be misspelled, or for math items, these could be wrongly placed decimal points or improper function signs.

Process of Elimination

For items with confusing choices, get rid of the obvious distracters so you can focus on the other choices. To select the best out of the remaining choices, make a judgment call.

Fill in the Blanks

Unless the CCO examination carries a right-minus-wrong scoring system, which is highly unlikely, do not leave any item unanswered. Guessing gives you a chance to score, but leaving a question blank will guarantee that you get a zero.

Test-Taking Commandments

For optimum performance during the CCO examination, remember these rules:

- Listen to the proctor for specific test-taking rules
- Ask the proctor if you do not understand the instructions
- Read and understand the instructions on the test paper
- Take note of the time allocation
- Give only one answer for each question
- Ensure that the answer corresponds to the question
- Mark the space for your answer as instructed
- Be aware of items you have skipped and return to them

- Double-check the answer sheet

- If you need to change your answer, erase the original completely

- Never communicate with other test-takers

- Do not panic

Sample Test Items

The following is a mini-practice test to help you identify distracters. Let your training, experience, judgment, and reasoning aid you in eliminating unseemly choices.

1. **50/20 = x. Solve for x.**

   a. 250

   b. 25

   c. 2.50

   d. 0.25

   Correct answer: C. The numerals *2* and *5* appear in your computation, but the decimal place tells the difference between right and wrong.

2. **A car costs $8900 with a 12.5% sales tax on top. What is the total price?**

   a. $8912.50

   b. $10012.50

   c. $18912.50

   d. $89125.00

   Correct answer: B. $1112.50 is 12.5% of $8900. Add that amount to the original $8900 and you have the total price. Watch out for distracters.

3. **There are 100 apples on the table for 55 inmates. Each inmate is entitled to one apple each. If a fifth of them decide not to take their share, how many apples will be left?**

   a. 56

   b. 55

   c. 46

   d. 45

   Correct answer: A. Choice D only provides the figure from which the final answer will be drawn. Choices B and C are distracters.

4. **"The mother is more taller than her son." What's wrong with this sentence?**

   a. the predicate

   b. the adverb

   c. the clause

   d. the punctuation

Correct answer: B. Adding *more* to the comparative adjective, *taller*, is incorrect.

5. **"Corrections officers are expectant to apply rules of grammer and punctuation in their reports." What makes the sentence wrong?**

   a. expectant

   b. grammer

   c. neither a nor b

   d. both a and b

Correct answer: D. Choice A (*expectant*, which describes an anticipating and excited feeling; *expected* is the right word) and Choice B (*grammer*, which is wrongly spelled), are correct.

6. **"Sitting upright at the desk, the study guide should be read in a well-lit area." What makes the sentence wrong?**

   a. the idiomatic expression

   b. the dangling modifier

   c. the subject

   d. the pronoun

Correct answer: B. There is neither idiomatic expression nor pronoun used in the sentence, and this makes Choices A and D incorrect. There is nothing wrong with the subject (*the study guide* is the subject here), which makes Choice C incorrect. Choice B is the answer because it is a dangling modifier that does not describe the subject properly, and which has nothing to modify in the sentence.

7. **If all entry-level corrections officers were expected to work "in the front line", what would rookies be doing on a typical day?**

   a. Acting as security specialists along the facility perimeter

   b. Paving all the roads leading to the gates

   c. Maintaining direct contact and communication with offenders

   d. All of the above

Correct answer: B. Based on the context of the question and the choices, the phrase refers to entry-level corrections officers being in direct communication and contact with offenders. It cannot be Choice A because *specialists* contradicts with the word *rookies* in the question; therefore, it is not basic and typical. Meanwhile, paving all the roads leading to the gates is a ridiculous choice, and this automatically invalidates "all of the above".

8. **Base your answer solely on this sentence: "Arson is the act of deliberately setting a human being on fire." Which phrase describes arson?**

   a. intentional burning of a person

   b. deliberate razing of buildings

   c. accidental firing of a gun

   d. none of the above

Correct answer: A. Although this is not the real and proper definition of *arson*, "intentional burning of a person" is the description assigned to it in the given sentence. By process of elimination, Choice D is ruled out because there is a possible choice. Meanwhile, Choice C is an obvious distracter. And while Choice B shows the actual meaning of arson, it is not in the the given sentence. This item is an example of following instructions to the letter, which relates to the actual CCO examination.

Part II: Crime and the U.S. Criminal Justice System

The primary objective of Part II is to familiarize you with the United States criminal justice system, from the time a crime is investigated until justice is served. The key points show the interrelationship among the police, courts, and corrections—and the law that binds them together.

Overview: The Nature of Crime

Crime is an act that violates an individual, a community, and/or the common good. Apart from being a direct physical threat to a person or property, crime threatens the general peace, security, and public order. A crime also threatens to inflict damage in the psychological, mental, emotional, environmental, economic, or moral sense. Due to its pernicious nature, crime is punishable by criminal law that falls within constitutional law. Punishments differ from one society to another, and it is the location where the law has been violated that perpetrators are tried.

Principal

In the United States, a crime is an offense committed by a person or a group of persons against another person or group of persons, or against the community. Technically speaking, only a human being can be a principal charged with a crime; a non-person that causes harm to a human being or to property cannot be held responsible for crimes. As stated in Title 18 of the US Code, principals of crime are not limited to the actual perpetrators (or actors):

   a) Whoever commits an offense against the United States or aids, abets, counsels, commands, induces, or procures its commission, is punishable as a principal.

   b) Whoever willfully causes an act to be done, which if directly performed by him or another would be an offense against the United States, is punishable as a principal.

Complicity

Crime also involves persons who commit complicity: those acting as accomplices and accessories, such as individuals who knowingly help the offender escape accountability and criminal liability, or those who deliberately obstruct justice where it should be served. In other words, aiding and abetting are criminal acts themselves.

Inchoate Crimes

Inchoate crimes (or preliminary crimes), which do not involve actual harm, are also punishable by law:

- Attempt, where a person threatens or tries to commit a crime but does not consummate it for some reason or other

- Solicitation, where a person commands or advises others to commit a crime

- Conspiracy, where a person agrees with another to commit a crime

Omission

Omission (a failure to act, which sometimes includes negligence) can also be considered a crime in situations where a person fails to deliver on the legal duty to take action that would otherwise have averted a dangerous or deadly incident involving person or property, or a disastrous impact on society.

An example of omission would be the deliberate non-payment of taxes. Another example would be neglecting to keep a sharp object away from a child's reach. If the child played with the sharp object, got cut by it, and bled to death in the process, the person who had left the sharp within the reach of the victimized child could be held liable. This act of negligence would be tantamount to wrongful death.

Punishments

Persons convicted of crime are meted out sentences as punishment. Incarceration, imprisonment, or "jail time" is only part of the sentence; others may be:

- Fine, which goes to the jurisdiction prosecuting the crime

- Restitution, which is paid to the victim (either a person or society as a whole)

- Community service, which is unpaid work

- House arrest (also called home confinement or home detention)

- Diversion, such as alcohol treatment or drug rehabilitation
- Alternatives within the provisions of law

Classifications of Crime

Felony

This is the most severe of the three criminal-offense types. Also known as index crime, felony has two categories: violent crime and property crime.

Violent crime, which is committed against persons or property, uses force or threat of force. It is composed of these offenses:

- Murder and non-negligent manslaughter
- Forcible rape
- Robbery
- Aggravated assault

Property crime, which involves the taking of money or property *without* the use of force or threat of force, is composed of these offenses:

- Burglary
- Larceny-theft
- Arson

Being crimes of the highest seriousness, felonies carry a minimum sentence of more than one year. The maximum punishment is life imprisonment for all states, except those that enforce capital punishment (the death penalty).

Felonies are sub-classified into four categories, as Classes A through D, with Class A warranting the maximum penalty for felonies.

Persons convicted of any crime falling under any of the felony classifications are called felons. After serving the prison term, they are legally stigmatized or subjected to discrimination. This stigmatization renders them constitutionally ineligible to do the following:

- Vote (under felony disenfranchisement)

- Access welfare, and certain public services and facilities
- Obtain federally funding housing
- Obtain professional and several types of business licenses
- Apply for jobs that require getting bonded
- Buy and be in possession of firearms, ammunition, and body armor
- Serve on a jury

Rescinding these exclusions depends on the jurisdictions where the felons have been convicted.

Misdemeanor

This is the second harshest of the three criminal-offense types, and can be considered a minor crime. Misdemeanors carry a minimum sentence of more than five days. The maximum punishment is one year.

Misdemeanors are sub-classified into three, as Classes A through C, with Class A warranting the maximum penalty for misdemeanors.

Common misdemeanors include:

- Petty theft
- Simple assault and battery
- Drunk driving without causing injury
- Disturbing the peace

Criminal mischief, which is a malicious and wrongful act against public or personal property, is typically a misdemeanor. This can be composed of defacement, vandalism, or destruction of property that is not arson. Each state has a different definition of misdemeanor.

Infraction

This is the least serious of the three criminal-offense types, and is sometimes called a petty offense. Infractions carry a maximum sentence of five days, and a minimum of "no imprisonment" that means an offender can be released without serving time.

Typical infractions include:

- Traffic-related violations, such as speeding and running a stop sign
- Jaywalking
- Littering
- Violating building code provisions
- Violating local laws and ordinances
- Exhibiting nuisance behavior

The Elements of a Crime

In criminal law, elements of a crime are used to prove—beyond reasonable doubt—that the suspects have committed the crime with which they are charged.

In the traditional and universal sense, elements of a crime involve such concepts as knowledge, intent, opportunity, instrumentality, system and motive. Correspondingly, for an act to be called or deemed criminal, and for this act to warrant legal consequences, it must be proven in courts that the actor possessed any or all the elements of a crime while the act was being carried out.

In the United States, there are two elements of a crime required for prosecution

Mens Rea

The Latin phrase for "guilty mind", *mens rea* describes the suspect's state of mind and culpable intent while s/he was in the process of committing the crime.

This concept is important in proving that a crime has been committed. Its attributes relate to adverbs describing the actor's commission of the crime: "purposely", "knowingly", recklessly", or "negligently".

Actus Reus

The Latin phrase for "guilty act", actus reus describes the suspect's engagement in the commission of a crime. *Actus reus* occurs when bodily movement has resulted in the injury or death of a living thing, or damage to property. However, omission that does not involve bodily movement has been legally described as an *actus reus* because of the failure to perform a duty prescribed by law.

Parties to a Crime

Parties to a crime are the individuals who commit the punishable act. Where one is the actual perpetrator that consummates a criminal offense, the others are support systems violating the law as well. Being such, they also constitute vicarious liability.

Principal

The principal is the individual who actually carries out the crime. The criminal liability of a principal depends on what law s/he has violated. Examples of principal roles include shooting a person, setting a house on fire, stealing money from the bank vault, and dispensing illegal drugs to a buyer.

Accomplice

The accomplice is an individual who helps the principal in carrying out the crime. For aiding and abetting the principal, an accomplice can be charged and convicted in the same manner as the principal. Examples of accomplice roles include serving as a lookout at the crime scene and driving the getaway vehicle.

Accessory Before the Fact

An accessory before the fact is an individual who initiates the idea of committing a crime, plans or helps plan, or orders the principal to carry out the criminal act. For aiding and abetting the principal, an accessory before the fact can be charged and convicted in the same manner as the principal. Examples of accessory-before-the-fact roles include masterminding an assassination, plotting a terrorist attack, and hiring a professional killer to murder a person.

Accessory After the Fact

An accessory after the fact is an individual who knows that a crime has occurred, then helps the principal, accomplice, and/or accessory before the fact avoid the hand of the law. The criminal liability of an accessory after the fact depends on the kind of participation in regard to the crime. Examples of accessory-after-the-fact roles include tampering with evidence, helping criminals elude capture, and harboring fugitives.

The related concept, misprision of felony, involves anyone who is aware that a felony has actually been committed, yet conceals the knowledge from the authorities. S/he is either slapped with a fine or imprisoned for not more than three years, or penalized with both.

Criminal Behavior

There are a number of conditions and circumstances, and combinations, that cause a person to commit a crime. Criminal sociologists and psychologists generally believe that these are either internal or external attributes.

Internal factors include genetic predisposition, lack of moral values, inability to temper negative emotions, and self-serving interests. For instance, certain individuals are driven to commit crimes because they are naturally violent, are unable to contain their desire to avenge an injury inflicted on themselves or their loved ones, or are too greedy to control their appetite for money and power.

External factors include the political, economic, and social climate. For instance, individuals are driven to commit crimes because they are disgruntled by government decisions, they are financially disadvantaged and are convinced that they have ho other means of fending for themselves or feeding their families, or they are bullied or ostracized in their respective communities.

Crime Prevention and Suppression

Efforts to control crime, if not eradicate it, call for the proactive participation of stakeholders that are not limited to the government and non-profit organizations, but also include the private sector (that is, commercial establishments, the community, the general public). Efforts include massive awareness campaigns on preempting youth to join gangs, reporting suspect activities in the area, and utilizing technology to inform the public on the effects of lawlessness, social disorder, and violence.

The Rights of Victims

Victims are at the receiving end of crimes. They are the ones harmed by the perpetrators even if they are not the actual targets of the criminal acts. Under the

Crime Victims' Rights Act, victims of criminal offenses punishable by federal laws are afforded such entitlements as:

- Right to restitution

- Right to be protected from the accused

- Right to be treated with fairness

The Evolution of Crime

Crime is a dynamic and ever-changing dilemma that adapts and conforms to the times. Although the result is the same (that is, to inflict harm on a person or damage to property), the motives and modus operandi evolve. The changes happen according to current environments, situations, technologies, and other factors like migration and globalization.

Hate Crime

Also called bias crime, this relatively modern phrase embodies various felonies committed against legally defined protected classes, or minorities classified by race, color, national origin, ethnicity, gender, gender identity, sexual orientation, or disability. Even amid the promotion of cultural diversity and heterogeneity, the United States suffers from a growing number of hate crimes.

Individuals who commit hate crimes possess an adverse attitude toward any of the protected classes, and are thus motivated by enmity and bias. They are so enamored by preconceived notions, stereotypes or discriminatory thoughts about a protected class that they are driven to commit aggravated assault.

The US Department of Justice (DOJ) and the Federal Bureau of Investigation have reported the prevalence of hate crimes across the country, with at least 130,000 hate crimes committed since 1991. Race is the leading bias motive, followed by religion and sexual orientation. The homeless status of an individual has also become an alarming bias motive; since the turn of the millennium, the number of assaults against homeless individuals in many states has risen.

Cyber-Crime

Another modern-day offense, cyber-crime involves the use of a computer and the exploitation of networks such as the Internet. The motive of cyber-crime actors is to harass or cause deliberate harm on their victims for different reasons, such as revenge, jealousy, vanity, and commercial gain.

Examples of cyber-crimes are hacking, fraud, identity theft, invasion of privacy, child pornography, and defamation. When committed with the use of a computer and the exploitation of a network, crimes like copyright infringement and intellectual property (IP) theft become acts punishable by cyber-crime laws.

Transnational Organized Crime

Also called transnational crime, transnational organized crime (TOC) involves a group of individuals who perform illicit activities across national boundaries. A typical TOC network is well-funded and highly equipped, and is thus operationally ready to commit more complex and violent acts, and to inflict collateral damage.

With globalization and easy travel from one country to another, many American offenders have engaged in TOCs that include human smuggling, trafficking of persons or body parts, drugs, arms, and exotic animals, as well the trade of stolen art and other valuables, counterfeit products, other contraband and cyber-crime.

Money laundering is a common criminal activity in TOCs because networks need to make their ill-gotten wealth seem like it was gained through legitimate business ventures.

Government corruption, especially in poor nations, is also pervasive in countries where TOCs need to be facilitated in executing criminal stratagems and schemes. Companies registered in the United States are checked for dealing in the corruption of foreign governments in order to conduct their businesses overseas, and are required to comply with provisions of the Foreign Corrupt Practices Act of 1977. These TOCs also have the potential to bring power and influence to individuals operating the networks, or to other beneficiaries like terrorist organizations.

American Law

American law is founded on the United States Constitution. Being "the supreme law of the land", the Constitution defines the limits of federal law and preempts conflicting laws promulgated in any of the fifty states, plus the territories. Any law that contains "unconstitutional" provisions are invalidated and scrapped, and should be repealed. It is the Supreme Court of the United States (or US Supreme Court) that resolves disputes on this matter.

The Laws of the Land

The Constitution

Since it was enforced in 1789, the US Constitution has been amended several times, beginning with the Bill of Rights. To date, it has a total of 33 amendments, including six unratified ones.

Federal Law

Federal law is a body of constitutionally valid laws enforced within federal jurisdiction. Essentially, it protects interests at the national level (such as foreign affairs, the military, interstate commerce, and the American economy as a whole).

The general and permanent federal laws are collected and compiled in the Code of Laws of United States of America (or the US Code, USC), and are sourced from federal statutes, treatises, court rules, administrative-agency rules, and case laws.

On international arrangements, the United States participates as a party to a host of treaties, agreements, and conventions that criminalize certain acts. It adheres to provisions in legally binding documents like the Geneva Conventions, Universal Declaration of Human Rights, and the International Covenant of Political and Civil Rights. The Secretary of State compiles, edits, indexes, and publishes the United States Treaties and Other Arrangements that, as prescribed by the US Code, serves as the legal evidence of the documents' existence.

Federal laws apply to anyone committing an offense in the United States and its territories. Examples include the Civil Rights Act of 1964, the Homeland Security Act of 2002, and the Digital Millennium Copyright Act (1998).

Common Law

This pertains to a system that relies on case law, previous judicial pronouncements, or law reports on prior decisions, rather than on legislative enactments, in formulating court decisions. All states subscribe to the common-law system except Louisiana (which uses a hybrid model combining English and French systems.)

State Laws

The state formulates laws based on its constitution, but these should be—first and foremost—compliant with the US Constitution. It also sources state-wide laws from statutes, court rules, rules of its agencies, and case law.

Local Laws

Local laws differ across jurisdictions within a state or territory, and usually deal with public order and safety. Examples include zoning ordinances and land-use regulations.

Juvenile Laws

Juvenile laws apply to minors—persons who have not reached the age of majority—who commit criminal acts. The age of majority and the age definition for juveniles vary from state to state. By and large, juveniles are tried in juvenile courts, distinct from that of adult courts. However, there are situations where minors are prosecuted as adults.

American Justice

The criminal justice system is society's response mechanism to crime. It is composed of institutions that prevent, control, suppress, and punish acts that violate criminal law. In other words, it is responsible for maintaining law and order in the community, as well as for penalizing and rehabilitating those who have been proven guilty of perpetrating the crime.

In the United States, the criminal justice system is not a single mechanism that oversees the entire population. Rather, it is a network of smaller, decentralized, and distinct criminal justice systems that work according to constitutional provisions and within their respective jurisdictions.

To wit: The federal criminal justice system is concerned with crimes committed within federal property or Indian reservations, while each state's criminal justice system deals with crimes committed within the geographic boundaries of the state.

Other criminal justice systems involve the local government (city, county, and/or township), military installations, or other special jurisdictions where there are specific enforcements procedures and responsibilities.

Like that of other countries, the US criminal justice system is triggered by the commission of a crime.

When a criminal incident takes place, the criminal justice system will run on an established set of processes performed by the following components:

- Police

- Courts

- Corrections

Criminal procedure and the administration of justice thus take place, covering such areas as:

- Law enforcement management (under police)

- Pretrial services (under courts)

- Arraignment and trial (under courts)

- Prosecution and defense (under courts)

- Pleadings

- Sentencing (under courts)

- Appeals (under courts)

- Probation (under corrections)

- Parole (under corrections).

Police

The front line of the criminal justice system, police (or law enforcement personnel) detect or receive reports of criminal incidents, and are the authority in investigating these.

Police officers (or law enforcers) obtain information and details from the victim, from witnesses, or from other persons who have reason to believe that a crime has been committed. When they have determined the veracity of the report, they follow through until they have solved the crime or declared the case closed.

The investigation process involves establishing motive, inspecting the scene of the crime and gathering evidence to support a criminal case and bring justice to the victim. More importantly, it seeks to identify and apprehend the actor, the suspect, and/or an individual suspected of having aided in carrying out the crime.

Law enforcers are authorized to arrest suspects and detain them, but only within the prescribed arrest procedures and within the period of time permitted by law. Without an arrest warrant, the police are allowed up to 48 hours to detain suspects.

Holding a person in police custody involves reading the suspected individual the Miranda warning, with very limited exception; otherwise, the police will have violated the person's right against self-incrimination (as provided for by the Fifth Amendment to the US Constitution), and court proceedings can be substantially undermined. The police can be held liable for this.

There is no specific format or wording for the Miranda warning. However, the typical content must clearly state concepts, including:

- The suspect's right to remain silent when questioned by the police

- The suspect's right to consult an attorney before answering any of the questions asked during the interrogation or police investigation

- The suspect's affirmation that s/he knows and understands all the rights as explained by the arresting party.

The police organization is structured as a bureaucratic pyramid with the head (or chief of police) holding the highest position. Deputies are next in the hierarchy, with specialized functions like managing administration and operations.

Patrol officers work beats on foot or in vehicles, and are in direct contact with members of the society that the organization protects.

Policing at the federal level has over five dozen agencies, with each enforcing a specific area of criminal law. The Department of Homeland Security and the DOJ are the largest law enforcement organizations in the United States.

The DOJ is the largest public law enforcement organization in the United States, with agencies including the Bureau of Alcohol, Tobacco, Firearms, and Explosives (ATF), the Drug Enforcement Administration (DEA) and the Federal Bureau of Investigation (FBI).

The FBI primarily functions as the agency that protects and defends the United States against terrorist threats. Its other function is "to enforce the criminal laws of the United States", generally pertaining to federal criminal offenses like trafficking explosives and blasting public property. The FBI's assistance may also be requested by state police agencies in investigating and solving crime.

Jurisdictions from the state level down to smaller units also have law enforcement agencies, such as the statewide police (except Hawaii), highway patrol, and sheriff's departments.

There are over 17,000 public law enforcement agencies across the country, with approximately one million full-time employees (including the 30% who are not sworn officers).

Law Enforcement Management

This pertains to organizational management, particularly administration and operations. It oversees the manpower and logistic capabilities of the police agency, and the proper and effective performance of functions.

Police agencies upgrade their logistics capabilities to conform to current standards. Technology is used to increase efficiency in dispatch, record keeping, and other detection and investigation procedures like DNA profiling.

In view of crime prevention and crime suppression efforts, the concept of community-oriented policing has been widely adopted to draw the public closer to the police.

Enhanced police-community relations enable the quicker resolution of many crimes because citizens are more trusting of law enforcers. In many cases, people have cooperated with the police willingly, even voluntarily giving sensitive information to help with the investigation of crimes.

Courts

The courts component of the criminal justice system initially determines whether or not the criminal case should advance to trial. The courts' role in the criminal justice system begins when the police component files a report (also called an arrest report), which contains all the relevant information on the crime investigation.

Like the criminal justice system itself, courts in the United States fall within specific judicial networks that are closely linked to one another.

Federal Courts

Federal courts hear cases regarding federal criminal offenses. Jurisdictions of federal courts are either geography-based, like the district courts for trial and the circuit courts for appeals, or subject matter-based like the Tax Court, US Foreign Intelligence Surveillance Court, and Court of Appeals for the Armed Forces.

The US Supreme Court is the ultimate unit of the federal judiciary. It has jurisdiction over all federal courts, as well as over state courts on matters of federal law. It is composed of nine justices, all of whom are presidential nominees that must be confirmed by the Senate. Of these, eight are associate justices and one is the chief justice who presides over oral arguments made before the court.

State Courts

State courts are established within each state's jurisdiction, and are overseen by the states' supreme courts. State courts are similar to the geography-based structure of federal courts, with district and appellate courts that hear criminal cases.

Territorial Courts

Territorial courts pertain to the district courts in the US territories of Guam, the Northern Mariana Islands, and the Virgin Islands.

Special Courts

Special courts pertain to adjudicative bodies on particular fields of criminal law. Examples include drug courts, appellate courts for military service members, and traffic courts. The administration of justice continues with court proceedings.

The Trial Process

Pretrial Services

Results of a police investigation are turned over to the district attorney's office, particularly to the prosecutor designated to represent the state and the victim of the crime. The prosecutor will make the decision whether to pursue the case. In making the decision, s/he considers the circumstances of the crime, weighs the merits of the arrest report and police investigation, and gives justifiable reason whether to press formal charges against a suspect.

If the prosecutor believes that the case would not prosper due to lack of evidence, or should be dropped altogether for some reason or other, the detained suspect should be released immediately.

Relatedly, a prosecutor who has already filed a formal charge with the court can declare *nolle prosequi*, which means that the case will no longer be pursued. In this case, the detained suspect should be freed from custody without unnecessary delay.

A suspect in a criminal case is entitled to a defense counsel, or an attorney that represents him/her. Indigent suspects who cannot pay for this legal representation will be assigned a publicly appointed defense counsel.

For a case to progress, a suspect is presented during pretrial, in which s/he makes a first appearance before a judge or a magistrate.

Arraignment

The arraignment stage is when the suspect (by now called a respondent) is formally read the document that charges him/her of a crime. In the presence of the prosecutor and the defense counsel, the respondent enters a plea of guilty (or *nolo contendere*, which means "no contest") or not guilty.

Regardless of the plea entered, the respondent (or defendant) will be made to face trial and receive adjudication.

Legally defined as either a natural person or individual, or an organization, a defendant is responsible for litigation costs and all other legal expenses, aside from fines and damages.

Depending on the jurisdiction, a defendant accused of, and charged with, a serious offense may not be allowed to post bail and seek temporary liberty. The judge bases his decision on this matter on several factors, to include the defendant's criminal history and propensity to commit crime while awaiting trial. If the judge has a reason not to grant bail, the defendant will be jailed throughout the legal process.

Also depending on the jurisdiction, a defendant may be required to attend a preliminary hearing, in which the judge determines whether or not there is probable cause to continue with the case. If the judge does not find any, the case will be dismissed. A defendant may also waive the right to this preliminary hearing, and proceed to the trial proper.

Trial

If there is sufficient cause to proceed with the trial, the defendant receives an indictment, which is a written statement of the charge against him/her. The indictment contains all the facts surrounding the crime and its corresponding criminal case. Trial on a criminal case is the process where the defendant is judged on whether or not s/he committed the crime.

It is not the judge but the jury, an independent body, that gives the verdict of guilty or not guilty, based on the evidence presented by the prosecutor against the defendant, and argument made by the defense. In no instance during and within the trial can and should a judge influence the jury and the outcome of the trial.

A jury consists of jurors, or people selected and summoned by the court to hear the facts of a specific case, then to look into the evidence that the judge deems legally admissible or worthy of being included in the trial.

Governed by established court principles and rules, the jury's role is to listen to arguments of both sides.

Prosecution and Defense

When the trial is in order, the prosecutor and the defense counsel become opponents (or adversaries) who are charged to defend their respective clients in order to win the case. The adversaries present their arguments and evidence. Evidence can consist of material to support the assertion that the suspect in a criminal case has, indeed, committed the crime. The testimony of witnesses is a common form of evidence.

Witnesses are persons who have actually viewed or heard the crime, or those who may not have been at the crime scene but who possess information relevant to the crime. They execute their testimony in writing, take oath, and affirm that they have given a truthful account. Otherwise, they can be found guilty of perjury.

Essentially, only pieces of evidence that are relevant, and which have probative value, are admissible in court. Those that have been admitted for presentation are marked, "Exhibit 'A'", then "B," and so forth.

Evidence of character that involves a defendant's reputation or opinion has little bearing in trying a specific case. Under normal circumstances, court decisions cannot be based on prejudice. For instance, a celebrity who openly admires the bravery of Adolf Hitler cannot be found guilty of bombing a public area just because he has given that opinion, and was physically present during the incident that police investigators hypothesize as having been carried out by a Nazi terrorist.

Pleadings

If the jury finds the defendant guilty beyond reasonable doubt and gives the verdict as such, s/he is convicted of the crime, and is meted out a sentence that the judge passes.

Of late, jury trials in the United States have been replaced by plea bargaining. In this court-approved process, the prosecutor and the defense negotiate and agree to settle on a case without having to undergo trial. The prosecutor gains a conviction because the defendant has voluntarily pleaded guilty to committing the crime, and saves court resources that would have otherwise gone to a long-drawn trial. In some instances, accused persons plead guilty to less serious charges, such as manslaughter instead of murder, in order to serve more lenient sentences.

There are cases where plea negotiation (or plea bargaining) has resulted in the non-incarceration—outright exoneration even—of defendants. Still on rarer occasions, plea bargaining has allowed convicts facing execution to make concessions in exchange for a life sentence with or without parole. While it has reduced the backlog in the courts and public expenditures related to criminal procedures, this out-of-court settlement is not always an effective alternative in serving justice.

Appeals

Convictions are not entirely final, in the sense that defendants have the right to appeal court decisions or the jury's verdict, and try to cause a reversal with an appeal.

When an appeal is made, a criminal appellate procedure begins and the defendant is treated as an appellant. As an appellant, the convict files with the appellate court an appellant's brief, a document that questions or argues the judgment, and which points out legal errors that have impacted the outcome of the case.

If the defendant is acquitted, which means that the prosecution and the crime victims have lost the case, no appeal can be made.

As guaranteed by the Fifth Amendment, defendants cannot be subjected to double jeopardy, or being prosecuted multiple times for the same offense. However, exceptions to double-jeopardy cases are those that fall under the dual and successive prosecution policy (or the Petite policy).

An appeal is not meant to present additional evidence or new witnesses; rather, it is a motion for the appellate court to review the facts and findings borne of the trial that has taken place in the lower court.

The decision by the appellate court can only be one of three:

1. Agree with the trial court and uphold (or affirm) its decision
2. Disagree with the trial court and reverse its decision
3. Agree in part and disagree in part, which means that the case will be sent back to the lower court for proper action.

Appellants who are not satisfied with the appellate court's decision may petition the United States Supreme Court to review the case one more time, for the last time. However, the chances of a case getting accepted for review are slim.

In any case, appeals take time to see final decisions. On average, these take eleven months to be resolved, although many stretch over years. Appellants who are sentenced with imprisonment remain convicts until their exoneration, if at all.

Sentencing

Courts follow sentencing guidelines, which are formulated to set standards and limitations in the imposition of sentence.

On the death penalty, capital crimes (or capital offenses) punishable by federal laws have been eligible for sentences of execution since 1988 when the 16-year moratorium was lifted. The Federal Death Penalty Act of 1994 enables capital punishment for almost all persons convicted of homicide. In reality, only half or less of verdicts chose the death penalty as a sentence.

Homicide cases include:

- Assassinating the US President or Vice President
- Killing US nationals in a foreign country
- Killing persons aiding federal investigations, including law enforcers and state correctional officers
- Murder of a federal prisoner
- Murder of escaped prisoners
- Retaliatory murder of a witness, informant, or victim
- Death resulting from hostage-taking or kidnapping incidents
- Death resulting from hijacking
- Genocide
- Conspiracy to murder

Other federal capital offenses include:

- Mailing of injurious articles with intent to kill, or those that result in death (even without the intent to kill)
- Large-scale drug trafficking

- Espionage

- Treason

There are 41 capital offenses listed in the US Code. Punishable by federal law, these are distinct from capital offenses punishable by laws of states that enforce the death penalty. Eighteen states plus Washington DC have abolished the death penalty statute:

1. Alaska	7. Maryland	13. New York
2. Connecticut	8. Massachusetts	14. North Dakota
3. Hawaii	9. Michigan	15. Rhode Island
4. Illinois	10. Minnesota	16. Vermont
5. Iowa	11. New Jersey	17. West Virginia
6. Maine	12. New Mexico	18. Wisconsin

Vermont has an exception – the state enforces capital punishment for treason.

The methods by which a prisoner may be executed vary by state:

- Lethal injections
- Electrocution
- Gas Chamber
- Hanging
- Firing squad

Clemency, Pardon or Reprieve

Convicted felons who are sentenced to death (or death-row inmates awaiting execution in an incarceration facility) may be granted clemency and released from prison. Public officials who are vested with the power to exercise leniency and show mercy to death-row convicts are usually the US president or the state governor.

Meanwhile, convicted felons (or inmates) who are not sentenced to death but who are also incarcerated may be shown mercy by public officials who are vested with the power to exercise leniency.

Such demonstrations of mercy or awards of leniency (clemency, pardon, reprieve) to inmates fall within the definition of administrative sentencing. These are not made by the judiciary; instead, the awards are given by the executive branch of government. In the administrative model of sentencing, officials of administrative/containment facilities (or correctional facilities) are authorized to control the length of sentences.

American Corrections

Corrections is the third component of the criminal justice system. A system in itself, corrections pertains to the management of individuals accused or convicted of crimes. It also relates to the network of public agencies and private institutions, as well as the programs and services that apply to the punishment and rehabilitation of inmates.

Correctional operations are mainly a concern of state governments and, as appropriate, the smaller jurisdictions, except for criminal cases at the federal level.

Management of individuals accused or convicted of crimes generally points to the direction of imprisonment (or incarceration). This means overseeing the confinement of persons in either prisons or jails within the court-specified or -prescribed period; thus the term "serving time".

The network of public agencies and private institutions includes correctional facilities, as well as government bodies that regulate rules and regulations on correctional administration and operations.

Correctional programs and services see to the inmates' well-being, and include the counseling of inmates and reformation of incarcerated individuals. By reformation, academic and vocational courses are also taught, with the hope that inmates released from incarceration and reintegrated into society will be skilled enough to find a job and earn a decent living.

Sample Test Items

The following is a mini-practice test to help open your eyes to distracters, as well as to assess your understanding of terms and concepts up to this point. Let your training, experience, judgment, and reasoning aid you in eliminating unseemly choices. Remember to follow each and every instruction – they will guide you in eliminating incorrect answers. Understanding the reading also leads to correct answers.

On vocabulary-building strategies, aside from making it a habit to look up words in the dictionary, using contextual clues in passages will enable you to get the meaning of the word, synonyms and antonyms, phrasal verbs, and verb-preposition or adjective combinations. It will also help you interpret figurative language and idiomatic expressions.

1. **Which sentence is incorrect?**

    a. The sun shined yesterday.

    b. The judge imposed a fine of imprisonment.

    c. The earthquake shook the ground.

    d. The island is bounded by waters.

Correct answer: A. Choice A is incorrect because of the grammatical error: The sentence should have used *shone* as the past tense of the verb "shine" that describes illumination. The use of *shined* pertains to cleaning and buffing surfaces of objects like shoes.

2. **Which sentence is incorrect?**

    a. The business thrived because of the owners' hard work.

    b. The rescue team dived into the waters to search for the missing body.

    c. He hanged his police officer's uniform to dry.

    d. She pleaded guilty to plagiarism.

Correct answer: C. The use of *hanged* as the past tense of the verb "hang" should be limited to persons being executed. In the sentence above, *hung* would be the correct past tense; that is, for clothes, paintings, and other objects. The verbs in

Choices A, B, and D were used correctly. In particular, *pleaded* in Choice D should not be used as *pled*.

3. **Which sentence is incorrect?**

   a. The sky is blue.

   b. The police handle public order.

   c. The sun rises in the west.

   d. The ocean is a body of water.

Correct answer: C. While all sentences are grammatically correct, Choice C presents a factual error; the sun always rises in the east. This tip does not apply to items that specifically instruct you to draw a conclusion from nowhere else but the passage supplied.

4. **Which statement can be easily verified?**

   a. A female fan initiates legal action, in which she accuses a male celebrity of raping her at 4 PM on Memorial Day four years ago, in a resort on the Caribbean.

   b. A female celebrity initiates legal action, in which she accuses an unknown male fan of burglarizing her apartment on Valentine's Day five years ago.

   c. Both a and b.

   d. None of the above.

Correct answer: A. Choice A presents concrete leads to an investigation because the police can check documents pertaining to the male celebrity's schedule and whereabouts around the time of the alleged rape. Choice B is a shot in the dark, entailing a tremendous amount of resources to find evidence that the burglary in the apartment was specifically committed by a male fan—and not just a random person. With Choice A being a possible answer, Choice D is stricken out. With Choice B being incorrect, Choice C is eliminated.

5. **Which statement correctly describes the US criminal justice system?**

   a. It is a network of distinct criminal justice systems.

   b. It is a network of offenders who cross national boundaries.

   c. Either a or b.

d. Neither a nor b.

Correct answer: A. The US criminal justice system is composed of smaller, interconnected justice systems.

6. **"The inmate got a secret message across by shoving another inmate, nudging the chaplain, and ignoring the corrections officer." Which part of the sentence pertains to a phrasal verb?**

   a. shoving another inmate

   b. nudging the chaplain

   c. ignoring the corrections officer

   d. getting a secret message across

Correct answer: D. Phrasal verbs, or phrases that demonstrate action, are verbs combined with adverbs, prepositions, or other grammatical elements. Choices D pertains to the phrasal verb, *get (something) across*.

7. **In Gaston Leroux's *The Mystery of the Yellow Room*, he writes: "The entire world hung for months over this obscure problem—the most obscure, it seems to me, that has ever challenged the perspicacity of our police or taxed the conscience of our judges." What is the antonym of *perspicacity*?**

   a. carelessness

   b. bluntness

   c. happiness

   d. worldliness

Correct answer: B. Knowing how to use contextual clues is helpful in looking for word meanings, as well as synonyms or antonyms. Although the passage itself may be insufficient to conclude from, the choices can offer hints. Perspicacity means sharpness, and bluntness is its opposite. Reading comprehension is part of the CCO examination and it is important that you understand the passages provided in the questionnaire.

8. **In Max Ehrmann's *Desiderata*, he writes: "Be yourself. Especially, do not feign affection. Neither be cynical about love; for in the face of all aridity and disenchantment, it is as perennial as the grass." In the simile, what is being compared to the grass?**

   a. affection

   b. aridity

   c. love

   d. yourself

Correct answer: C. A simile is a figure of speech that compares an object with a completely unrelated object. It functions like a metaphor, except that a simile uses connective words that include *as* and *like*. Choice C ("love", which is represented by the pronoun *it*) is the object being likened to grass.

9. **Which statement best supports the concept of *age of majority*?**

   a. It varies from state to state.

   b. It is achieved when almost half the population is old.

   c. Neither a nor b.

   d. Both a and b.

Correct answer: A. As written in this study guide, the *age of majority* is the age when a person is no longer to be considered a minor or a juvenile. The exact age depends on the state where the person is prosecuted, which makes Choice A correct. Choice B, a ridiculous statement, has never been implied in this study guide, and thus invalidates Choices C and D.

10. What does statute of limitations prescribe?

    a. provisions of law that limit geographic boundaries of states

    b. prescribed time for initiating legal action

    c. minimum number of witnesses for the defense

    d. maximum amount of admissible evidence

Correct answer: B. Choices C and D do not represent any legal concepts, while Choice A does not properly define the phrase, which makes Choice B the correct answer. Skim through the pages of a legal dictionary to understand concepts and minimize guessing.

11. What is antonymous to Class-A felony?

    a. heinous

    b. illustrious

    c. serious

    d. all of the above

Correct answer: B. The operative word, *antonymous*, in the question spells the difference between right and wrong; miss it and you shave a point off your score. Choices A and C, being synonymous to a Class-A felony, correspondingly invalidate Choice D and leave Choice B as the only possible correct answer. Enriching your vocabulary by reading extensively, and by looking up words in the dictionary, helps you understand concepts better.

12. Which phrase ineffectively describes international laws?

    a. International laws are bound by conventions, treaties, or agreements signed by two or more countries.

    b. The United Nations is only one of many supranational organizations where international laws originate.

    c. The United States adheres to several of these.

    d. The Universal Declaration of Human Rights is a comprehensive compilation of international laws that promote hate crimes.

Correct answer: D. The sentence in this choice is ridiculous.

13. Which statement best supports the concept of crime?

    a. Felonies are serious offenses that all warrant maximum punishment, such as execution or life imprisonment.

    b. For an act to be punishable by law, it has to have resulted in a person's death or injury, or property loss or damage.

    c. The prevention and suppression of crime is as much the responsibility of the police as it is of the general public.

    d. The United States is so advanced that all crimes have evolved such that no offender uses a primitive modus operandi anymore.

Correct answer: C. Notice that Choices A, B, and D have words and phrases like *all*, *has to have*, and *any more* that limit the possibility of correctness in the statements. To explain, not all felonies warrant maximum punishment, only some; not every act punishable by law has to have resulted in loss of life and property; and not all crimes committed in the United States use state-of-the-art technology to carry out crimes. Choice C is the only logical answer to the question. A thorough grasp of basic concepts in your profession makes it all the more important for you to return to your training materials and the knowledge acquired through experience.

14. Which choice best describes this passage: "In imposing a sentence to a term of imprisonment for a felony, the court may include as part of the sentence a requirement that the convict be placed on a term of supervised release after imprisonment"?

    a. Imposing a sentence is not required of all felons.

    b. Part of the sentence is required of the convict.

    c. Supervised release is an option in a sentence.

    d. The court excludes a convict's imprisonment.

Correct answer: C. Choice C summarizes the statement in the passage that the court may include supervised release in the sentence. This item encourages the use of reading comprehension and critical analysis skills. Choices A, B, and D are ridiculous.

15. There were 720 hate crimes committed in Year X, which precedes Year Y. If the annual increase in hate crimes is projected at five per cent (5%), how many hate crimes will there be at the end of Year Y?

    a. 720.5

    b. 725.0

    c. 755.5

    d. 756.0

Correct answer: D. Five per cent (5%) of 720 is 36. Add that to 720 (number of hate crimes committed in Year X) to get the figure for Year Y, which follows the base year.

16. There were 507 acts classified as transnational organized crimes (TOCs) in Year 1, which immediately precedes Year 2 that, in turn, is followed by Year 3. If the annual increase in TOCs is projected at three per cent (3%), how many TOCs will there be at the end of Year 3? Round off the answer.

    a. 538.0

    b. 537.0

    c. 523.0

    d. 522.21

Correct answer: A. The instruction to round off the answer instantly eliminates Choice D, which is not a whole number. To compute for the yearly increase, first get the 3% of 507 (Year-1 figure); the exact answer is 15.21. Do not round this off yet because the fractional part can increase the next-step answer. Add 15.21 to 507 to get the tentative answer that represents the Year-2 figure: 522.21. Next, get the 3% of 522.21; the exact answer for this is 15.6663. Again, do not round this off yet as the fractional part can increase the final answer by one whole number. Add 15.6663 to 522.21 to get the new tentative answer that represents the Year-3 figure: 537.8763. Eliminate Choice C, which is another distracter, and pick the right answer from Choices A and B. This is where the rounding-off procedure comes in: the fractional part, .8763, adds one whole number to the figure. Therefore, the correct answer is Choice A.

Part III: The American Corrections System

The primary objective of Part III is to refresh you on the workings of the American corrections system, and on its evolution – that is, from its long-ago purpose of mere punishment and incapacitation of criminals, to what it is today. The key points show challenges and opportunities in the rehabilitation process that criminal offenders go through.

Overview: The History of Corrections

Before *corrections*, the term *penology* was widely used to describe the US prison management system. This was before the 1960s—actually beginning in the 1700s—when the process was viewed more to as a strictly punitive affair, rather than a rehabilitative action. Penology in those days was thus focused on punishing convicts and deterring further criminal activities by fleshing out the banishment and incapacitation of convicted felons.

Prison-warden routines mainly involved receiving, counting, clothing, and feeding the prisoners, preventing them from disturbing the peace and causing trouble in the facilities, and ensuring that the premises were well-maintained and well-guarded to avoid incidents of escape.

Above that, prison wardens enforced the convicts' sentences of confinement within the penitentiaries, banishment from society, and incapacitation to engage in further criminal activity. They oversaw the prisoners' hard labor, an inherent part of the penalty. In those days, the typical demonstration of authority involved toughness and intimidation. Prison wardens were trained to view prisoners as incorrigible criminals who could no longer return to their benevolent ways, and whose lives had ended the moment they thought ill of others and victimized the community with their crimes.

Reform initiatives eventually made it possible for penology to take a more humane and forward-looking course, not only to benefit the inmates' well-being *per se*, but society as a whole.

The punishment and crime-deterrence aspects continued to be priorities in prison management; sanctions and measures in this regard remained in strict enforcement. Yet, at the same time, efforts would be channeled towards restoring the prisoners' inclination to good conduct, and instilling in them moral values and a sense of self-worth.

Little by little, administrators of penal institutions turned their operations from reactive to proactive, with the intent of preparing the prisoners for productivity and self-sufficiency. Depending on the ingenuity of directors and their managers, penal institutions would institute livelihood programs like agribusiness and handicrafts production. The new philosophy would be embraced by practitioners; individual approaches, shared throughout the penology field. The small successes in correcting the behavior and outlook of prisoners eventually became constant and widespread.

Although this generally applied to those with lighter sentences—those who still had an out-of-the-pen future to look forward to—the reform process did not exclude prisoners who were meted out the death penalty, life imprisonment without parole, or other longer-term sentences. In 1974, the United States Congress created the National Institute of Corrections "to provide training, technical assistance, information services, and policy/program development assistance to federal, state, and local corrections agencies."

Apart from that, each state has established its own corrections department. Where other states use "Department of Corrections", preceded by the name of the state (eg, Alabama Department of Corrections and Wyoming Department of Corrections), the following states have their own variations:

- California Department of Corrections and Rehabilitation
- Connecticut Department of Correction
- Delaware Department of Correction
- Hawaii Department of Public Safety
- Idaho Department of Correction
- Louisiana Department of Public Safety and Corrections
- Maryland Department of Public Safety and Correctional Services
- Massachusetts Department of Correction
- Nebraska Department of Correctional Services
- New Mexico Corrections Department
- New York State Department of Correctional Services

- North Dakota Department of Corrections and Rehabilitation
- Ohio Department of Rehabilitation and Correction
- Tennessee Department of Correction
- Texas Department of Criminal Justice

Incarceration

Imprisonment or incarceration—a consequence of criminal actions—is synonymous with "(justly and lawfully) putting people behind bars". This is the process of committing convicted felons to incarceration or correctional facilities that are mandated and maintained at the federal, state, local, and special jurisdictional levels.

Over time, prisoners and convicts began to be called *inmates*; even the term *criminals* has evolved to *offenders*.

The general types of correctional facilities are:

- Prisons
- Jails

Prisons

Federal and state prisons are facilities for inmates who are serving sentences that exceed one year. Facilities within the prison system are designed to minimize inmate escape. As such, these have thick perimeter walls layered with barbed wire that are normally electrified, armed watch towers, heavy lighting systems, CCTV monitoring systems, and motion sensors.

Inside a prison facility, there are additional layers of security that further contain the inmates within their designated blocks, cells, or units. These structures restrict movement and interaction with other groups of inmates. This aims to prevent conspiracy among themselves, or outbreaks of violence against one another.

Segregation is based on gender (male and female), although there are cases where specific prison facilities also need to segregate by race due to the escalating incidence of racially motivated violence. This further segregation commonly involves blacks, whites, Latinos, Asians, and individuals of other color.

Ideologies and religious beliefs, which have already caused many alarming incidents inside correctional facilities, also entail the separation of inmates who espouse conflicting opinions.

Administrators periodically review the situations in their respective institutions, and rework the segregation policy as necessary to maintain order and safety on the premises. For instance, placing Jewish and neo-Nazi inmates together in a single unit can bring more harm than good. Unspoken provocations or spoken threats can easily erupt in violence.

In the context of age, adults are ideally separated from juveniles because it is believed that the latter should have their own set of facilities and differently structured rehabilitation programs. However, due to the rise in juvenile crime since the mid-1990s, correctional facilities designed for adults already accommodate juvenile inmates. This means that youth will not enjoy the relative leniency accorded to them, and will be subjected to the same rules and policies imposed upon the adults.

Upon incarceration, convicted felons take diagnostic tests. They also undergo risk assessment based on their criminal record, medical history, and other indicators that will determine their propensity to threaten peace and order inside the facility. The evaluations are made in order for administrators to determine how inmates should be grouped together to achieve a more secure, peaceable, and productive environment within the facility.

Relatedly, facility-safety evaluations are conducted periodically based on the inmates' overall behavior. For example, the Federal Bureau of Prisons (BOP) factors the "rate of assaults" into the process, and this is by determining the number of serious and less serious assaults occurring for every 5,000 inmates. The BOP has the following inmate security classifications within the federal corrections system:

- High
- Medium
- Low
- Minimum

Names assigned to inmate security classifications vary by state, local, or special jurisdiction. In some jurisdictions, the custodial levels are further subdivided; inmates within a security classification are further categorized according to restrictions, privileges, and freedoms. Accordingly, federal prison-security levels are classified as follows, from the least to the most extreme (that is, in terms of inmate security risk):

- Minimum
- Low

- Medium

- High

There are a total of 119 variously classified federal prisons across the BOP-designated regional divisions: Mid-Atlantic Region, North Central Region, Northeast Region, Southeast Region. South Central Region, and Western Region. As of December 2013, these federal prisons house 215,482 inmates and employ 38,948 staff.

At the state level, there are over a thousand differently classified prisons that accommodate male and female inmates. Some of these are exclusive to a gender, while others have been designed for mixed placements.

Minimum Security

This classification pertains to prisons that accommodate inmates who pose the least risk of inflicting physical harm on others, damaging property, and/or causing trouble during the incarceration period.

Most inmates in minimum-security prisons are white-collar offenders whose felonies have not involved homicide, violent sex offenses, or kidnapping. Most likely, they have committed tax evasion, fraud, or other non-violent crimes that are punishable all the same.

Because of the very low security risk, facilities are built with minimal fencing. The dormitories are non-secure, although they are locked at night. These prisons have low staff-to-inmate ratios, with the staff experiencing few and isolated incidents of inmates' assaultive and disruptive behavior, or attempts to escape.

Minimum-security programs include community-based work assignments, and are usually carried out in conjunction with the local government. Examples are cleaning up roads and public areas, planting trees, and assembling light structures like playground equipment. Inmates do not require supervision, and are allowed privileges like access to the Internet, TV, and/or radio, and use of the Internet, mail, and visitations.

Such federal facilities are called Federal Prison Camps (FPCs). There are five FPCs nationwide. Of these, four are for male inmates; two, for females. Another federal minimum-security is the Morgantown Federal Correctional Institution (FCI) in West Virginia.

In federal jargon, the difference between an FPC and an FCI is generally the housing type. Where FPCs have dormitories, FCIs have cells. Additionally, FPCs have very limited or no perimeter controls while FCIs have wired fences.

State facilities vary in name, and some have specialized functions that cater to different needs. There are those that house inmates who are geriatric, mentally ill, or in need of drug rehabilitation. There are also treatment centers for substance abuse (including tobacco dependence), and co-ed motivational boot camps.

Low Security

This classification pertains to prisons that accommodate inmates who pose a slightly higher security risk than their counterparts booked in minimum-security facilities.

Facilities are built with double-fenced perimeters, and accommodate inmates in dormitory and cubicle-housing structures. Correspondingly, the staff-to-inmate ratios are slightly higher than those of minimum-security prisons. Such federal facilities are in most FCIs that are run by the BOP, and Correctional Institutions (CIs) that are privately managed. There are 21 low-security FCIs and 14 CIs nationwide.

Medium Security

This classification pertains to prisons that accommodate inmates who pose a higher security risk than their low-security counterparts.

Facilities are built with double-fenced perimeters that have electronic detection systems, and which are watched over by armed guards. These facilities accommodate inmates in dormitories or cell-type housing. Correspondingly, the staff-to-inmate ratios are higher than those of low-security prisons, and there are tighter internal-control measures.

At the federal level, there are 28 medium-security FCIs and three medium-security US penitentiaries (USPs). These medium-security facilities are adjacent to minimum- to low-security Satellite Prison Camps (SPCs) that provide inmate labor within the main campuses, or community service within the locality. At the state level, there are over 400 medium-security facilities for male and female inmates.

High Security

Also referred to as closed custody, this classification pertains to prisons that accommodate inmates who pose the highest security risk. The term "max prisons" is associated with this type of incarceration.

Inmates in high-security prisons are those whose crimes have involved killing other people or inflicting serious physical harm on others, and severely damaging property.

Due to the pernicious nature of the crimes for which most inmates have been convicted, the facilities are enclosed within thick perimeter walls made of stone or concrete, and reinforced with wire fences and escape-detection devices. The perimeter also features watch towers with heavily armed guards and powerful lighting systems.

The facilities have markedly high staff-to-inmate ratios, and correctional officers are intensively trained to anticipate and contain violence and attempts of escape.

Housing consists of multiple- or single-occupant cells, grouped into blocks or clusters, that have exclusive toilets and showers to prevent inmates from mingling with one another and stirring up trouble.

Many cells are electronically controlled so corrections officers can avoid being in contact with extremely dangerous inmates. Activities in these units are monitored 24/7, with the use of a complex network of surveillance systems. Inmates are thus deprived of their privacy.

At the federal level, there are six high-security penitentiaries in four of the BOP regions: Atwater USP (California), Big Sandy USP (Kentucky), Canaan USP (Pennsylvania), Lee USP (Virginia), Lewisburg USP (Pennsylvania), and McCreary USP (Kentucky). Minimum-security SPCs are attached to all these high-security USPs.

At the state level, there are over 300 high-security prisons that accommodate male and female inmates.

Supermax

With the evolving nature of crime, the "super-maximum security" sub-classification has been given to modern-day prisons that house the most notorious, most predatory, most uncontrollable, and most threatening offenders.

These convicted felons have demonstrated that they can pose utmost security risks on the national and international scale—without remorse and regard for human life.

Conditions at supermax prisons are harsh, and more punitive than rehabilitative, even to the point where activists have shown concern about the inhumaneness applied to the inmates. This is being continuously studied in order that the American corrections system can achieve a balance between the inmates' human rights and society's right to safe and secure communities.

There are several supermax prisons across the United States that are run by state governments. These exclude Alcatraz (or "The Rock"), which ceased its three-decade operations in 1963. Currently operational supermax prisons in the United States are located in Federal Correctional Complexes (FCCs), which are campuses that have facilities for different security classifications.

The most secure—in the country and in the world—is the Florence Administrative Maximum Facility (ADX, ADMAX) in Colorado. Located within the Florence FCC, it houses 411 male offenders that include terrorist bombers, spies, mobsters, and serial killers.

Some of the most infamous criminals incarcerated at Florence ADMAX are Zacarias Moussaoui, Ramzi Yousef, Theodore John "Ted" Kaczynski, and Robert Philip Hanssen.

Moussaoui had pleaded guilty to half a dozen felony charges, all of which were conspiring to commit acts that would culminate in the 9/11 attacks. Being rendered by the presiding judge ineligible for the death penalty, he was sentenced to life imprisonment without the possibility of parole (LWOP).

Yousef had pleaded guilty to crimes connected with perpetrating the 1993 bombing of the World Trade Center in New York. He also took responsibility for conspiring on the Bojinka Plot that had included an assassination attempt of Pope John Paul II during the Roman Catholic head's visit to the Philippines, and the bombing of United Airlines and Delta Airlines flights originating from Thailand. He was sentenced to 240 years for the bombing *plus* another LWOP term for the death of a Japanese national as a result of bombing a Philippine Airlines flight.

Kaczynski, commonly known as The Unabomber, was convicted of heinous crimes connected to the spate of domestic bombing campaigns that he carried out at universities in seven states and on an American Airlines flight. He was sentenced to LWOP.

Hanssen, a former FBI agent, was found guilty of selling American government secrets to the Soviet (now the Russian) government. He was sentenced to LWOP.

Florence ADX was designed and built as a lesson learned from a series of security lapses in other USPs. The turning point was the twin incidents at the Marion USP in Illinois on 22 October 1983. That day, inmate Thomas Edward Silverstein fatally stabbed Corrections Officer Merle Clutts several times. Hours later, Silverstein's fellow inmate also murdered Corrections Officer Robert Hoffman using the same stratagem of exploiting lax security policies and procedures.

Although afforded state-of-the-art technology to maintain the tightly controlled environment, and highly trained and armed guards to secure the premises, Florence ADX is not spared from untoward incidents caused by the inmates, individually or in cahoots with others. In 2013, three members of the prison staff were injured when an inmate attacked them with a crude weapon.

Solitary Confinement

There are occasions when inmates need to be isolated and placed in cells that, in federal prisons, are called Special Housing Units (SHUs).

In most of these instances, inmates are deprived of privileges to make any contact or form means of communication with other people, including staff. This is because they have exhibited predatory behavior, proclivity to stir violence in the facility, or willingness to participate in gang activity (like trafficking drugs and weapons in the facility).

Placement in the SHUs may be short-term or long-term, depending on the facility's policies and evaluation procedures. However, there are other instances when inmates need to be isolated because they are subject to threats by other inmates.

The principle of managing prisoners through solitary confinement was the basis of the Pennsylvania system (or the separate system), which was conceived in the mid-1800s and adopted by hundreds of prison facilities around the world.

Death Row

Within the federal corrections system and in states where capital punishment is enforced, inmates who are meted out capital punishment await execution, or those awaiting the overturning of their appeal on their death sentence, are placed on "death row". In the United States, there are various facilities with the death row. At the federal level, there are the Terre Haute FCC in Indiana that houses male prisoners, and the Carlswell Federal Medical Center in Texas.

Other Prison Facilities

The federal prison system lists other facilities that accommodate inmates with different security classifications.

These facilities include:

- Detention centers, BOP-managed or privately run
- Federal Transfer Centers (or FTCs)
- Administrative facilities.

Jails

Informally called lock-ups or slammers, jails are locally operated incarceration facilities that hold individuals on a shorter term; that is, up to one year. Jail inmates may be persons awaiting trial or sentencing, and are not necessarily convicted felons.

There are almost 800,000 jails in counties, cities, tribal territories, and other jurisdictions across the United States. Some are government-managed while others are privately run.

Probation and Parole

Probation

Probation describes the status of sentenced offenders who are given reprieve from incarceration and a relatively limited level of freedom. As opposed to incarceration (imprisonment or jailing), probation is a corrections measure administered under community supervision.

The federal and state criminal justice systems take probation as a sentencing substitute for incarceration, and this is left to the discretion of the judges.

Probation may be granted to offenders whose imprisonment sentences are suspended and not carried out at all, or to those whose incarceration is cut short for reasons like good behavior.

Individuals who are given the status are called probationers, and they are subject to the periodic monitoring and evaluation of corrections authorities (specifically, probation officers who are sometimes known as community supervision officers).

Probationers who are in violation of any of the conditions laid out by the courts will suffer the revocation of their freedom, and will likely be slapped with imprisonment. Violation of the terms of probation is a crime *per se*.

The periodic monitoring and evaluation of probationers runs throughout the court-determined duration of the probation. Supervision made by the probation officers involves the assessment of the probationers' behavioral progress based on legitimate rules and requirements.

Standard rules and requirements for probationers include:

- Not being in possession of firearms
- Reporting to probation officers as scheduled
- Submitting to substance-abuse tests and treatments
- Performing community service as directed

In some instances, probationers are ordered to abide by a curfew, maintain decent jobs and ensure the payment of taxes, reside at court-appointed dwelling and not move without permission, and/or not to leave the jurisdiction at any time.

Those who have a history of drug use or substance abuse are usually compelled to attend and participate in treatment programs.

The types of probation are:

- Intensive supervision
- Standard supervision
- Unsupervised

Intensive Supervision

Although not technically incarcerated, probationers undergoing this program are granted very limited freedoms, and are closely monitored. They may be placed under house arrest—confined for extended periods (with or without the liberty to leave home for short, monitored trips)—and be fitted monitoring devices.

Since 1983, the US criminal justice system has been using monitors to address certain issues, particularly the overcrowding of correctional facilities.

The technology-aided supervised release of probationers was marked by ankle bracelets (also called tethers) that relied on radio frequency, until such time as electronic monitoring (EM) tags were developed. These EMs, still strapped around the ankle, provide real-time tracking via the Global Positioning System (or GPS).

Standard Supervision

Probationers undergoing this program are ordered to report regularly to their designated probation officers and carry out tasks that they may be required to do. Depending on what is prescribed, their modes of reporting may be in person, through telephone, or by snail mail that bears a postmark.

Unsupervised Probation

As the term suggests, probationers under this program do not need to report periodically to probation officers. Normally, they only need to submit themselves at the end of the probation term. However, they must prove they have fulfilled the requirements, which may include paying fines and court fees within a time limit.

Examples of celebrities slapped with criminal charges and sentenced to probation include Robert Downey, Jr., Lindsay Lohan, and Martha Stewart.

Downey, Jr. had been charged with possession of illegal drugs (cocaine and heroin) and a revolver, and was sentenced to a 36-month probation. In a separate incident, Lohan was found guilty of possession of cocaine, among other crimes, and would also be sentenced to a 36-month probation. When he violated his probation, Downey Jr was put in jail for half a year. And when Lohan violated hers by missing the mandatory court hearing and nine court-ordered treatment classes for alcohol abuse, she was incarcerated for three months and made to attend a rigorous inpatient rehabilitation program.

Meanwhile, Martha Stewart was sentenced to a five-month federal incarceration, plus a 24-month probation immediately following it. This was after being found guilty of, among others, conspiracy (to commit securities fraud) and obstruction of justice. For five months within the probation period, Stewart was ordered to be confined at home with limited time to leave the house. She was also compelled to wear an EM tag for a period within her house arrest.

There are over four million probationers across the United States. Statistically, about 60% of them are expected to complete the terms of probation with permanent success. The rest are incarcerated for violating conditions of probation, and will most likely face imprisonment.

Parole

Parole is the provisional release of a prisoner from incarceration due to good behavior, statutory mandates, or other justifiable reasons. As opposed to incarceration (imprisonment or jailing), parole—much like probation—is a corrections measure administered under community supervision.

Parole differs from probation in that it technically constitutes freedom from incarceration; the incarceration period has ended.

Unlike probation, parole is not a substitute for serving time inside correctional facilities. But like probation, parole may also entail supervision, in which designated parole officers periodically conduct checks on their wards.

Inmates who are and granted parole are called parolees. Those who are serving a life term are also considered for parole, unless they are sentenced to LWOP.

Parole is a privilege, not a right. The eligibility for parole is considered and determined by an authority, such as the parole board, that has jurisdiction over the inmates' incarceration.

Among the basic requirements is the parolees' declaration of a residential address as his home during the parole period. This will be verified by the authorities, and the assigned parole officer can visit every now and then, announced or unannounced, to see if the parolee is conducting himself or herself accordingly.

When parole is granted, a parole certificate is issued as a statement of conditions that the parolee must satisfy within the prescribed time. Violations of any of these conditions can lead to revocation and, consequently, to the parolee-in-question's return to incarceration. Conversely, demonstrations of good behavior can get parolees discharged earlier than scheduled.

Parole statuses include "active" and "inactive", according to the degree of supervision administered on a parolee. Actively supervised parolees are made to report to their parole officers regularly in person, by telephone, or by mail. Inactively supervised ones are those who have complied with the conditions in the parole certificate before the end of the parole term.

According to the US DOJ, about 45% of parolees successfully complete their sentence and get reintegrated into society as free individuals. The rest go back to prison or have absconded.

Criminal Sentencing

Some of the terms and concepts below expound on sub-topics in the latter part of Chapter 2. These are emphasized here because of their significance to corrections.

Clemency

This pertains to the award of leniency or a show of mercy to an inmate, given for various reasons and under different circumstances. The privilege to grant clemency does not rest on the judiciary (the courts); rather, it is an exercise of discretion by the executive (federal, state, or other jurisdictional administrators). Clemency is synonymous with a pardon that is given by the pardoning official, and usually—but not always—leads to the convicted felon's release from prison. It can also mean downgrading the sentence to a less harsh penalty.

It must be noted that clemency cannot be equated with the nullification of the conviction, in which the guilt of an inmate is reversed and stricken off the record as though s/he has been innocent all along. In other words, although some inmates may be granted clemency and released from prison, their records still reflect their conviction.

Commutation

This pertains to the downgrading of sentence severity, for a host of reasons like clemency and appeals on the length of the sentence. One example is when the US President commutes the death sentence of a federal prisoner to LWOP. Another is when a governor commutes the LWOP sentence of a state prisoner to a basic life sentence; that is, one with the possibility of parole.

Reprieve

This pertains to postponement or temporary cessation of the incarceration process due to reasons like advancing an appeal for sentence commutation. Other reasons are compassionate and medical. An example of compassionate reprieve would be when an inmate is allowed to leave the correctional facility, usually escorted, to attend the funeral of next of kin. An example of a medical reprieve would be when an inmate is allowed to leave the correctional facility, usually escorted, to seek treatment for an illness.

Good Conduct Time

Also called good time credit or time off for good behavior, good conduct time pertains to calculations made to reduce incarceration sentences. Generally, inmates who demonstrate what the law describes as "exemplary compliance with institutional disciplinary regulations" are credited with up to 54 days each year, depending on the currently enforced rules and regulations, and this credit shortens their time served.

Theoretically, inmates sentenced to ten years can expect their incarceration shortened by up to 540 days (or almost 1½ years) if they do not subject themselves to disciplinary action. Good conduct time may be subject to disciplinary disallowance, or altogether forfeited, if inmates violate prison rules and regulations before the vested date (or the day of crediting).

Recidivism

In criminal justice, recidivism is defined as a former offender's relapse into criminal activity, behavior, or habits. It is officially measured by his or her actual return to incarceration facilities or community supervision within three years of serving time.

Manifestations of recidivism include deliberate violations of probation or parole conditions, and commission of a new crime. The resulting action encompasses re-arrest and reconviction, re-incarceration to those previously put behind bars or first-time incarceration to those who have had the privilege of probation.

A report by the Bureau of Justice Statistics (BJS) implies that more than half of the released and discharged convicts become repeat criminals (or recidivists), most of whom commit robbery, burglary, and theft. These commonly committed crimes may be due to disabling conditions in the outside world, particularly economic incapacity. For instance, a lot of released prisoners find it hard to be employed because they are stigmatized. This is why they commit robbery, burglary, and theft. However, there are other recidivists who have an inborn inclination, or acquired propensity, to crime.

Habitual-offender Laws

Informally called three-strikes laws, habitual-offender laws are enacted at the federal and state level as a deterrent for repeat criminal offenses. These laws impose stiffer punishments to persons who have been previously convicted twice. On the third commission of a criminal act, twice-convicted offenders are slapped with mandatory life sentences, some without parole, notwithstanding the nature or gravity of the latest crime.

After Texas enacted its habitual-offender law in 1974, the following states have followed suit (not in chronological order):

- Arizona
- Arkansas
- California
- Colorado
- Connecticut
- Florida
- Georgia
- Indiana
- Kansas

- Louisiana
- Maryland
- Massachusetts
- Missouri
- Montana
- New Jersey
- New Mexico
- North Carolina
- North Dakota

- Pennsylvania
- South Carolina
- Tennessee
- Utah
- Vermont
- Virginia
- Washington
- Wisconsin

In Connecticut and Kansas, habitual offenders are called persistent offenders. In Missouri, they are called prior and persistent offenders.

Some states' habitual-offender laws have been amended since, with reforms in mandatory sentencing to increase the efficacy against recidivism.

Rehabilitation: Challenges and Opportunities

In corrections, rehabilitation is the means of achieving a goal in criminal justice: to enable the ideal reentry and reintegration of incarcerated or community supervised convicts into society. By ideal reentry and reintegration into society, the criminal justice system envisions released prisoners, as well as discharged probationers and parolees, as fully rehabilitated and reformed individuals.

Effective rehabilitation methods will have shaped them into morally bound, non-violent members of the community. These will have completely reversed their statuses as public-safety threats and transformed them into productive citizens.

Over 95% of incarcerated persons are ultimately released, with the remainder staying in prison for life or being cast into death row. Of those released, 80% will be on parole, and the rest are completely free. Not many of them are afforded opportunities to start their lives all over again, thus the staggering number of recidivists.

Of late, criminal justice experts have been contending that substandard, flawed, and weak correctional processes, as well as transitioning approaches are the main culprits in the ever-increasing recidivism rate.

Broadly speaking, current correctional processes and transitioning approaches are holistic in nature. They attempt to redevelop the individual's physical, psychological, and spiritual wellbeing. Programs are educational, vocational, and self-improvement to give them confidence in rejoining the work force. Amid the challenge in numbers, many jurisdictions institute reforms and innovate according to the times and evolving needs. Successful implementation equates to reduced recidivism.

A few important innovations have given new meaning to some well-known concepts:

- Shock therapy
- Regimented Inmate Discipline program
- The Sheridan model

Shock Therapy

Also referred to as shock incarceration, shock probation, or shock parole (whichever is appropriate), shock therapy is no longer a cruel electroshock therapy administered to the mentally ill. Now, it refers to a constitutional system of at once sanctioning and rehabilitating prisoners, probationers, or parolees—boot-camp style. It puts emphasis on self-discipline, treatment (particularly of substance abuse), and life skills.

Incepted in 1983, the therapy adopts the military way of instilling a sense of accountability and responsibility, especially among first-time offenders and juvenile delinquents. It focuses on drill and ceremony, strict adherence to protocols and schedules, rigorous physical training and activity (including hard labor), regular counseling and psychological intervention, and life skills-enhancement.

The quasi-military regime involves treating "shock" participants like plebes at military schools, organizing them into squads or platoons, and forcing them to espouse a highly controlled and monitored way of life. The shock factor is the force in behavioral change until such time as the wards have reworked their mind-set and rethought their moral outlook.

Contrary to what critics say, however, shock therapy does not tolerate capricious or retaliatory punishment on any participant who errs or falls short of the disciplining standards. The practice of shock therapy in itself has rigid guidelines. It undergoes an eligibility and selection process, which usually disqualifies high-risk and violent applicants. Some do not allow offenders charged with sexual offenses or those with psychiatric disorders, mental instability, and specified physiological problems. The program accommodates males and females.

Depending on the jurisdiction, shock therapy can run between 180 days and a full year. The mandate to participate comes from sentencing authorities.

Shock therapy is reminiscent of the New York-incepted Auburn system that was used as a prison model in the nineteenth century. However, the modern-day approach is more humane and apace with the times.

Regimented Inmate Discipline (RID) Program

The RID program is a more formal name given to shock incarceration. It is an alternative to imprisonment, and a strict way of transitioning prisoners into free individuals. The first RIDs were instituted in 1983, almost simultaneously in Georgia and Oklahoma. In 1987, New York launched its own, and other states followed. These pioneering RIDs were initially designed for the adult inmate population, but as time passed, the program philosophies were adopted to cater to juvenile needs.

A basic feature of RIDs is the emphasis on rewards rather than penalties; motivation and incentive are the key concepts that enable participants to rise to different challenges and assignments. Sanctions are also given but these are more physical (like push-ups) than measures like deprivation of certain privileges or solitary confinement.

A typical RID unit is housed in a contained facility surrounded by a barbed-wire fence, and participants reside in open-type dorms. Each unit has a staff organization headed by a manager, and filled by an administrative clerk and/or a secretary, case managers, counselors, correctional officers, and drill sergeants and/or instructors.

Regimented discipline extends beyond following a strict schedule, which involves waking up before dawn for physical exercises. Participants are also required to undergo elaborate ceremonies, including getting their heads shaven upon intake. Like military cadets, they memorize forms of address by which to call staff, know when to stand at attention, and mess (eat) with limited time and opportunities to socialize.

The RID program culminates in graduation ceremony, which their families are invited to attend.

Correctional officers involved in RIDs are generally supportive because the program has many satisfactory outcomes. Most of them think that the stringent measures are effective in making participants reexamine their lives, commit to a better way of life, and wear the confidence necessary in rejoining the outside world.

Overall, implementation of the RID programs has partly solved prison overcrowding and, correspondingly, the cost of operating prisons across the United States.

In case participants drop out of their RID programs, they are returned to the general prison population.

The Sheridan Model

A by-phrase in the corrections field, the Sheridan model relates to the rehabilitation program developed by the Sheridan Correctional Center in Illinois. Operated by the Illinois Department of Corrections, the medium-security adult prison facility for males is dedicated to the treatment of substance abuse.

Because of the comprehensive, multidisciplinary approach, Sheridan records a constantly low recidivism rate of 16%. Owing to the system of introducing and upholding best practices in criminal justice, the facility now takes the distinction as a landmark in the history of correctional reforms.

The Sheridan model exhibits keenness on confidence building, promotion of a positive attitude, and propagation of social responsibility (through properly mediated peer influence) among participants.

More than 75% graduate from the program, and a good number of them boast of obtaining at least one vocational certification. This reflects an effective campaign in transitioning the inmate-participants toward freedom and reentry into society's mainstream. As an added motivator, administrators attest to the character of deserving graduates and sign employment recommendations. They also provide job referrals and placement services.

Unlike shock therapy, the Sheridan model is "softer", "friendlier", and less military-like in method and technique. For instance, it calls units *families*, instead of *squads* or *platoons*.

The rehabilitative component includes educational programming, job training, anger management, parenting skills, and other therapies. The program runs for up to 36 months, with a further 90-day outpatient aftercare to ensure the full treatment of substance abuse. For their voluntary participation in the intensive substance abuse treatment, over half of Sheridan inmates are incentivized with credit that is applicable toward good conduct time. Statistically, this translates to a yearly average of 19 years of reduced incarceration, or an annual savings of $2.78 million in prison expenditure.

The cost-effective Sheridan model addresses prison overcrowding, among other issues in corrections.

The State of Corrections

The population under the control of the US corrections system is divided into two: the institutionalized and the community supervised. In 2012, about 2.23 million sentenced convicts were put behind bars (prisons, jails, or similar facilities). They represented an incarceration rate of 0.716% (or 716 inmates for every 100,000 of the entire US population), which is the highest documented figure in the world.

States with the highest incarceration rates were Louisiana, Mississippi, Alabama, Oklahoma, and Texas. States with the lowest incarceration rates were Maine, Minnesota, and Rhode Island. Of the number locked up in prisons, a total of 113,605 were women. Meanwhile, 551,154 were blacks; 500,604 were whites; 332,202 were Hispanics; and the rest were of other races. Of the 2.23 million, 159,520 were sentenced to life, and almost 31% of them were slapped with LWOP. Inmates in adult prisons also included minors, despite the establishment of the juvenile justice system. In that period, over 4.79 million people were subjected to community supervision as probationers or parolees.

In view of alarming incarceration rates that have resulted in overcrowded jails and prisons, the criminal justice system has opened itself to privately operated institutions that provide the same services as any public correctional facility. Corrections administrators from different jurisdictions have taken to outsourcing the services to commercial establishments. However, the $5-billion prison industry, which is ideally a cost-effective measure of easing the growing burden, has been criticized for several reasons:

- Absence of public accountability
- Use of the inmate population in forced labor, such as in the production of commercial goods that the prison-industry players profit from
- Under-staffing and skimping on facility security budgets
- Low wages and inadequate benefits for corrections officers.

A report by the BJS states that the cost-effectiveness promised by contractors has not materialized since the prison industry began privatizing in the 1980s. Many privatization contracts stipulate an occupancy guarantee, meaning that taxpayers pay almost the same amount for low incarceration rates as they do for full prisons.

Kentucky, the first state to subscribe to full privatization in corrections, discarded the practice in 2013.

Sample Test Items

The following is a mini-practice test to encourage you to recall what you have read in the study guide so far, analyze situations based on your readings, and turn to reference materials (including the dictionary) to familiarize yourself with terms and concepts.

As emphasized earlier, you must learn to identify the distracters that question-writers deliberately include in the choices.

1. **Which sentence is correct about jails?**

   a. Jails are not for females.

   b. Jails can accommodate people who are actually innocent.

   c. Jails should provide a death row.

   d. Jails will not hire staff from penitentiaries.

   Correct answer: B. Choice B is correct because jails book individuals who are awaiting trial or sentencing; meaning, even those who will later be found innocent by the courts are detained there.

2. **Which of the following statements is absolutely true?**

   a. Prison facilities accommodate criminal offenders who are sentenced to incarceration of more than a year.

   b. Jail time must exceed a decade.

   c. Probation is neither an obligation of society nor an honor for inmates.

   d. Parole is both a right and a privilege.

   Correct answer: A. Choice A is correct. The other choices do not demonstrate mastery of corrections or an understanding of language. Choice B is incorrect because the legal definition of *jail* is the facility where sentences shorter than one year are served. Choice C is not an absolute truth, while Choice D is false.

3. **Which is correct about Federal Correctional Complexes?**

    a.   These are strictly for women.

    b.   These may not cater to juvenile offenders.

    c.   These do not need any type of fencing.

    d.   These have more than one security classification.

Correct answer: D. Choice D is correct. The other choices do not fit the description of FCCs.

4. **Why are the most dangerous criminals eligible for supermax prisons?**

    a.   Supermax prisons are designed to avert security threats that felons convicted of heinous crimes can pose.

    b.   The amenities are provided specifically for religious extremists who are deemed America's most dangerous criminals.

    c.   The best psychologists are employed here to correct the predatory behavior of the most dangerous criminals.

    d.   The surveillance systems are also fitted with weapons to shoot prisoners who stir up trouble.

Correct answer: A. Choice A is correct. The other choices are irrational.

5. **Which concept is not directly related to clemency?**

    a.   award of leniency

    b.   executive privilege

    c.   inactive supervision

    d.   show of mercy

Correct answer: C. Choice C is correct because *inactive supervision* of probationers or parolees does not affect, or is not affected by, the granting of clemency or pardon to an inmate. Choices A and D are synonymous with clemency, and Choice B defines its nature - an administrative gesture and not a judicial proceeding.

6. **Which statement falsely describes probation?**

    a.   Inmates on death row cannot be eligible for probation.

    b.   Only probation officers have the power to grant probation.

    c.   Electronic monitoring devices track probationer activity.

    d.   Probation terms can be reduced, extended, or forfeited.

Correct answer: B. Choice B is correct because it falsely describes the implementing rules and regulations of probation. Choices A, C, and D are all true.

7. **What is the formal term for the day when good conduct time is credited?**

    a.   compassionate reprieve date

    b.   inmate calculated credit date

    c.   release date

    d.   vested date

Correct answer: D. Choice D is the correct technical term for the specified day when calculated good conduct time is credited and made enforceable. Choices A, B, and C are all distracters.

8. **Which statement is incorrect?**

    a.   Corrections engages in the administration of criminal sentences that require incarceration, probation, or parole.

    b.   Incarceration has alternatives.

    c.   Probation is not a substitute for incarceration.

    d.   Parole may be actively or inactively supervised.

Correct answer: C. Choice C shows the incorrect statement about probation. Choices A, B, and D are all factual statements.

9. **What word pertains to escaping probation or parole?**

    a.   abscond

    b.   estoppel

    c.   indictment

    d.   omission

Correct answer: A. Choice A is correct. Choice B, although a legal term, has nothing to do with the discussion on corrections. Choices C and D are terms in criminal justice, but do not describe the act of escaping probation or parole. It must be noted that Chapter 3 does not expound on the concept of a sentenced felon's absconding – but earlier in the guide, you were told to look up unfamiliar words in the dictionary, and make a habit of cross-referring to external sources to gain a deeper understanding of terms and concepts. Make sure you do!

10. **Which statement is true about robbery and burglary?**

    a.   These are interchangeable legal words.

    b.   Each has a meaning and implication distinct from the other.

    c.   Neither is a common crime among recidivists.

    d.   Both are practiced by all recidivists.

Correct answer: B. Choice B is correct: *robbery* describes the violent act of permanently depriving someone else of his or her property, as with a grocery store stickup, while *burglary* implies an intention to take other's property without necessarily being violent in carrying out the act. This explanation nullifies Choice A. Meanwhile, Choices B and C are contrary to Chapter 3. Again, this sample item is aimed at encouraging you to use refer to the dictionary and other sources to understand terms and concepts in criminal justice.

11. Which term is not within the concept of community supervision?

    a.   probation

    b.   parole

    c.   prison

    d.   tether

Correct answer: C. Choice C is correct because prison falls under incarceration. Choices A and B are the obvious terms relating to community supervision, and Choice D is a device used in tracking many probationers and parolees.

12. What challenge is common among released prisoners?

    a.   stigmatization

    b.   sanction

    c.   reformation

    d.   protocol

Correct answer: A. Choice A is correct because released prisoners are typically stigmatized as criminal offenders, or typecast as potential public-safety threats who will not do the community any good. Choices B through D are ridiculous.

13. What factors will make an RID program fail?

    a.   hard labor and physical training

    b.   schedules and protocols

    c.   drill and ceremony

    d.   capricious and retaliatory punishments

Correct answer: D. Choice D is correct because capricious and retaliatory punishments are not called for in the implementation of RID programs. Choices A through C, including hard labor that may give a false impression of unconstitutionality and inhumaneness, are fundamental elements in shock therapy and RID programs.

14. Which statement best describes shock therapy?

    a.   New York was the first to ban shock therapy in corrections.

    b.   Inmates on death row are thoroughly educated on the pros and cons of

        choosing the electric chair as a method of execution.

    c.   The Sheridan model of shock therapy is mandatory at the federal and state levels.

    d.   The RID program closely relates to shock therapy.

Correct answer: D. Choice D is correct; the rest are factually incorrect.

15. Which word pair best describes the overarching goal of the corrections system?

    a.   release and recidivism

    b.   punishment and rehabilitation

    c.   law and order

    d.   judiciary and executive

Correct answer: B. Choice B is correct because punishment and rehabilitation are what the corrections system ultimately tries to achieve. Choice A is ridiculous. Choice B is a general notion that does not fit the ideals of corrections, while Choice D only pertains to the branches of government that may oversee corrections processes.

Part IV: Your Career as a CCO

The primary objective of Part IV is to deepen your understanding of the corrections profession, for which you are about to be credentialed and certified. The key points show how corrections administration and operations are ideally carried out toward the goals of criminal justice.

Overview: The Corrections Profession

"33-3012" is the occupational employment code that the Bureau of Labor Statistics has designated for corrections officers. The classification, which includes jailers and law enforcers primarily assigned to correctional institutions, summarizes the job description as:

> " Guard inmates in penal and rehabilitative institutions in accordance with established regulations and procedures. May guard prisoners in transit between jail, courtroom, prison, or other point...
>
> Corrections officers are responsible for overseeing individuals who have been arrested and are awaiting trial or who have been sentenced to serve time in a jail or prison."

The basic, routine duties are streamlined as follows:

- Maintain peace and order in the facility
- Supervise and monitor inmate activity
- Evaluate and report on inmate progress
- Assist in inmate rehabilitation and counseling
- Help ensure that the facility keeps its standards

In some jurisdictions, corrections officers are called booking correctional officers/sergeants, detention officers/deputies, deputy jailers, jailers/jailors, or public safety officers. Generically, they are referred to as peace officers.

As of mid-2013, the corrections industry has a work force of 432,110, and is expected to grow by 5% in ten years. The number is distributed in the federal, state, and local settings. There are also corrections officers employed in facility support services, as well as psychiatric and substance abuse hospitals.

Of these, the highest-paying employer is the federal executive branch, with an annual mean wage of $53,240. The least-paying is facility support services, which posts an annual mean wage of $36,940. In 2012, the median pay is $18.74 per hour.

The work environment is expectedly dangerous because of the criminal nature of the individuals that corrections officers deal with. It is also stressful due to several factors, including 24/7 schedules that are usually divided into rotating eight-hour shifts. Being required to work overtime is not unusual.

Like counterparts in law enforcement, corrections officers are more prone to injuries because of their exposure to violence, including assaults directed at them. Ironically, while aware that inmates can exhibit irrational behavior, corrections officers are discouraged from delving deep into criminal records and familiarizing themselves with their wards' histories.

The degenerate and unhealthy state of several facilities, particularly inadequate security measures and lack of necessary equipment, increases the risk.

There is no gender bar in the profession, and it is normal for female corrections officers to be assigned to all-male, maximum-security prisons. Additionally, age is neither a deterrent nor an excuse for any corrections officer to be assigned to the most dangerous units within an incarceration facility.

To illustrate: On February 21st, 2000, a female corrections officer named Jeanette Bledsoe carried out her routine death-row duties at the Terrell Unit (now the Allan B Polunsky Unit), a prison operated by the Texas Criminal Justice Department. She had just escorted inmate Ponchai Wilkerson to the cell after his recreation, and was walking handcuffed Howard Guidry back to his, when the two men sprang from their supposedly secure positions and nabbed her. Bledsoe, 57 years old at the time and already a grandmother, would be taken hostage at knife-point for the next twelve-plus hours. This was until anti-death penalty activists were called to negotiate. The lady prison guard was eventually released, unharmed, after Wilkerson and Guidry had expressed their grievances.

The issues caused by, and arising from, this incident were the call for a stay in executions; administrative delays that affect inmate welfare, including delays in changing visitation lists; and the sorry state of conditions at Terrell.

The sorry state of the facility, as exemplified by the weak lock that Wilkerson broke in order to get out and restrain Bledsoe, underscored the insecurity and high danger level in the corrections work environment. Also, the fact that the death-row inmate possessed a deadly weapon, in this case a homemade knife, showed lax security checks in what was then classified as a medium-security prison.

Professionalism

The Rights and Responsibilities of a CCO

Like an entry-level corrections officer, or any member of the work force for that matter, you are entitled to rights and privileges. These include competitive salaries and typical employee benefits, such as leave, insurance, and retirement coverage.

Profession-specific benefits include clothing allowance for prescribed uniforms, opportunities for training and continuing education, and the eligibility for promotion to supervisory and administrative positions.

With regard to responsibilities, it is important to remember that you have obligations under the law, as detailed in the organizational policy, and that you must strictly comply with all the rules and regulations set forth by the institution where you work.

Where you perform your tasks in an official capacity and conduct yourself dutifully, yet encounter unfortunate incidents, the investigation that follows will determine the cause and your liability.

To illustrate: You respond to a violent altercation during visiting hours and, in the process of breaking up the fight, severely—although not deliberately—injure a visitor. Consequently, the visitor lodges a complaint against you.

Whether it is a personal liability that you will be answerable for (maybe because you have breached protocols in responding to emergency situations), or it is the institution's liability that the administrators will assume (maybe because there were no protocols instituted at all), will be determined during the ensuing investigation.

Conversely, if you conduct your duty according to policy, but are caught in a legal battle because of it, you are entitled to a level of immunity from complaints or lawsuits. This is as long as you have strictly adhered to policy.

Examples of conditions where you may incur personal liability while on duty include discriminating against inmates and depriving them of services because of their color, gender, sexual orientation, or other such attributes; acting indifferently or negligently during emergency situations that result to irreversible damage or death; and denying your charges their right to due process.

Core Values

As integral parts of the criminal justice system, corrections officers are expected to uphold non-negotiable life and professional values. Every organization has a unique value system, but the following list reflects the standards among corrections officers:

- Discipline
- Responsiveness
- Integrity
- Vigilance
- Ethics.

Code of Ethics and Professional Conduct

Ethics are the moral foundations of individuals and the institutions they represent. These closely relate to professional conduct, which must be becoming at all times. If ethics are not espoused, both the corrections officer and the facility that s/he works for will fail in the mission to promote peace and order not only within the premises, but in the community as a whole. Like any organizational policy, the code of ethics and professional conduct must be strictly subscribed to by correctional officers within and outside of their work environments.

Corrections officers are persons of authority who should command respect, not demand to be feared and possess self-entitlement. They are sworn to ensure public safety and security by keeping their units violence-free and policy-abiding, but never in the brutal and inhumane sense. Thus, they are compelled to act ethically.

Violating the code is tantamount to sanctions. Corrections officers who are at fault undergo investigation and hearing. The gravity of their unethical act determines the judgment. In the most severe administrative cases, punishments range from suspension to dismissal from the services. If a criminal act is involved in an incident, the case will be elevated to the courts.

A common example of breach of the code of ethics and professional conduct would be condoning associates to exhibit unbecoming behavior, such as maintaining sexual relations with inmates. A more harrowing example, which is criminal in nature, would be permitting (or just turning a blind eye to) a prison gang to operate a racket that involves smuggling drugs into the facility.

Core Skills

Even as you advance in your career and are given greater responsibilities, the application of the following general skills will remain necessary:

- Language
- Mathematics
- Clerical
- Observation
- Interpersonal
- Administrative and management

Language Skills

Communication is an integral part of your job as a corrections officer. A good command of the language, plus a wide vocabulary, enables you to convey your message accurately, and helps you establish more effective professional and social relationships.

Spoken English is the medium used for interacting with different sets of people: your superiors, peers, and subordinates; people who play supporting roles in corrections (such as health workers and social workers); people who do business with your facility; and members of the community in general. In any case, being articulate and coherent in conversation is a must for corrections officers. Speaking with clarity and conviction is crucial for disciplining, reforming, and negotiating with inmates.

Meanwhile, written English is the medium used for formal correspondence and inmate documentation. Accuracy, clarity, coherence are important in this case, especially in recording incidents, filing reports, and submitting assessments and evaluations.

Language skills also cover grammar, spelling, and punctuation, as well as reading comprehension and listening comprehension.

Reading comprehension is a tool for understanding, interpreting, and analyzing written material during problem-solving and decision-making processes. It also aids in compliance with laws, institutional policies, and facility standards.

Listening comprehension is your building block for successfully observing your surroundings, monitoring inmate activity, and making better evaluations on inmate behavior and recidivist tendencies.

Mathematical Skills

Math skills are important in completing routine procedures, such as determining the value of an inmate's personal property during intake, calculating bond percentages, bookkeeping, and so forth.

The practical application of arithmetic operations in your advancement to CCO can translate to computing for large quantities and complex mathematical problems. It is also necessary in resolving issues and making decisions within your assigned unit.

Clerical Skills

A corrections officer is not limited to securing premises and preventing violent outbreaks. They must also perform intake documentation, record-keeping, filing and submission of various types of reports, and evaluating inmate progress. Clerical work follows logical processes, including arranging files in alphabetical or chronological order, completing administrative forms with accuracy and truthfulness, and doing inventory work on facility and inmate property.

Additional clerical abilities include proficiency in computer programs that create and format documents and charts, process and organize inmate data, and produce informative and engaging presentations. The ability to use the Internet, especially for research purposes, is also essential.

Observational Skills

In actual situations, observational skills involve the five senses (where applicable) in order to have a clear, objective understanding of what is going on. However, during the CCO certification exam, only the sense of sight is needed to answer questions pertaining to a photograph or image. But even in this case, all the minute details must be noted and stored in the memory as precisely as these have been viewed.

To illustrate, below is a photograph taken by the National Aeronautics and Space Administration (or NASA) in 1963. It features astronauts engaging in tropical survival training, an important exercise to prepare them for any eventualities like an aborted launch or a wayward entry back into earth that could land them in the wilderness.

Note that for test items of this nature, your task is to view a separate sheet that contains the image. Study the subject and background carefully, within the time allocation (usually ten minutes.) When the time is up, you will be instructed to turn to the answer sheet and respond to the questions accordingly.

Remember that you will not be allowed to return to the image-in-question. Counterclaim your answers using your memory. Again, what is being tested here is the ability to recall facts and information objectively, as events you are investigating unfold or occur. The rationale for this is testing your ability to take in information as it comes, your keenness in processing details with your five senses and your accuracy in reporting on the situation.

From left to right: Unidentified trainer with astronauts Neil Armstrong, John H Glenn Jr, L Gordon Cooper, and Pete Conrad. Public-domain photograph from NASA

The test questions referring to the photograph may include:

- How many are present?

- How many non-whites?

- How many males?

- How many females?

- What are the people in the photograph doing?

- What kind of footwear are the people wearing?

- In what sort of place are the people gathered?

(Is it a jungle, a   field, or a rooftop?)
schoolhouse, a football

Observational skills have practical application in duties like inspecting people and objects, monitoring inmate activities and behavioral patterns, and detecting suspicious body movements and spoken lies. Tiny security lapses, such as failing to observe that a visitor has left something between pages of a book in the reading room, can lead to catastrophic outcomes.

Interpersonal Skills

Interpersonal skills build upon communication skills, as well as positive personality traits like firmness of belief and purpose, cheery disposition, trustworthiness, genuine concern, and social preparedness. With inmates, correctional officers must demonstrate interpersonal skills to sustain rehabilitation programs that call for face-to-face interaction, one-on-one conversations, and group discussions.

Outside of the system, corrections officers maintain proactive relationships with community stakeholders, and interpersonal skills are essential to delivering great results. On certain occasions, officers deal with such segments of society as the media that may want to feature the facility's accomplishments in criminal justice, or with academics that undertake research on breakthrough approaches in penology and rehabilitation. On other occasions, they visit schools and tell students what it is like to work in corrections.

Interpersonal skills are also manifested in distance communication, such as responding to official inquiries via telephone or e-mails.

Administrative and Management Skills

Administrative and management skills are not solely for the director and his or her immediate staff at the facility. These are also what corrections officers must hone, because they are, in their own way, administrators and managers. They steward the inmates to permanent reform and rehabilitation, and this is by disciplining their wards, rewarding them, boosting their morale, and seeing to their welfare.

To achieve their goals in supervising inmates, corrections officers exhibit leadership qualities. They set the example of obeying rules and regulations, following instructions, complying with standards, being trustworthy, and maintaining integrity. They also show the ability to coordinate inmate activities and programs with success.

Administrative and management skills require familiarization with the institution and the corrections system itself, critical thinking and analysis of situations that range from mild to severe, deductive and inductive reasoning, and decision making.

It is not uncommon for corrections officers to face challenges within their units, and it is usually up to them to resolve issues and solve the problem. To do this, they let policy guide them in their decisions. In more demanding instances, they elevate matters to their superiors. But in doing this, corrections officers are expected to narrate the background, circumstances, and the perceived gravity of the problem, to give details in full, to present higher authorities a set of alternate courses of action, and to justify their recommendations.

Correctional Operations

Thorough familiarity with corrections standards and facility procedures ensures the smooth flow of routine activities, and the proper execution of contingency plans.

Corrections officers are accountable for any deliberate action or inaction that compromises the integrity of the facility and the corrections system.

Compliance with Corrections Standards and Facility Procedures

Strict adherence to policy is crucial. Corrections officers must follow instructions to the letter, as with filling out checklists and forms as completely, carefully, and accurately as possible. A small infraction, a minor lapse, or a seemingly harmless omission can result in irreversible damage to all stakeholders—including the corrections officers themselves. The basic categories covered by corrections standards and facility procedures include the following:

- Physical plant (the facility's perimeter fence, offices, housing area, other structures)
- Personnel administration and management
- Inmate population discipline and supervision
- Security of facility, personnel, inmates, other persons involved in overall operations
- Services (food, medical, sanitation, hygiene, rehabilitation)
- Programs and activities.

Facility rules and regulations are put down in writing, and personnel are usually required to sign the documents as proof that they have received copies of the policy, and/or have read these and understood the stipulations fully.

Inmate Intake

The tasks involved in admitting, receiving, and booking inmates include documenting and verifying personal information, creating a central file that also contains an inmate's criminal record and nature of incarceration, conducting an inventory and valuation of the inmate's property, and marking these for storage, as well as getting the inmate to submit to the required drug, neuro-psychiatric, and physiological testing, and seeing to inmates' security designation, custody classification, and housing assignments.

Inmate Release

The tasks involved in processing inmates for release include verifying release orders and other pertinent documents, attesting to the proper and complete turnover of inmate property, and identification of the inmate to be released.

Inmate Counts

The routine counting of inmates many times a day and at bedtime, within the cell blocks or in activity areas, ensures that no inmate is missing for any reason, or has escaped the facility. If there is an incomplete count, corrections officers are compelled to file a report and submit to an investigation.

Inspections

Security and maintenance checks are conducted on facility premises and structures (exterior and interior), equipment and supplies, other material relevant to the workplace, inmates and their cells, visitors and their belongings, vendors and other persons. The routine includes assessing the conditions of cell locks and restraining devices (natural wear and tear or altered conditions), window bars and all exit points, medical-emergency stations and equipment, and mail matter that may contain controlled, flammable, toxic, or hazardous substances.

Mail

Inmates are allowed to receive mail, as long it is checked for prohibited items and the messages are censored. They are also permitted to send personal letters, which will be subject to censorship. Corrections officers are obliged to receive official and legal mail, and be sure that addressee-inmates receive and act on it in a timely manner.

Visits

Every facility has a policy on visits made to inmates. Normally, inmates' family members, lawyers or other fiduciaries, friends and other pre-screened persons are allowed. Corrections officers strictly implement visiting schedules and protocols, including visitor screening (regardless of gender or age) to check for prohibited items.

Drills and Simulations

Emergency-evacuation drills (like fire and earthquake drills) are carried out regularly to prepare staff and inmates for any eventualities, such as natural calamities. Corrections officers are taught how to organize and contain inmates during emergencies, and instruct them on how to stay safe.

Patrols

In higher-security correctional facilities, patrols are conducted by armed personnel along the perimeter. These are usually undertaken on marked vehicles, and some require the deployment of canine teams. Inside the buildings, particularly in the housing units, patrol teams are more frequently active from midnight to daybreak. The schedules vary to avoid predictability, and the aims also include confirming that no inmates are medically distressed.

Searches of the Person

Personal searches, also known as "searches of the person" are legal so long as they satisfy requirements within the constitutional guarantees under the Fourth Amendment, and are carried out within the rules of the criminal justice system. Theoretically, these searches are predicated on probable cause.

The basic aims of searches of the person are to stop contraband items from being smuggled, to detect inmates' possession of weapons and controlled substances, and—in less ordinary cases—to gather evidence of crime within the facility.

Searches of the person are not limited to inmates. Such preventive measures apply to practically all persons entering the facility, regardless of ethnicity or stereotype. Thus, these may also be conducted on staff, service-providers and visitors, to restrict anyone's capacity for undertaking illicit operations.

These procedures may be preceded by such search modes as the use of metal detectors, and must be documented according to the facility's rules and regulations. The following are the types of searches of the person:

- Patdown search
- Clothed-body search
- Strip search
- Body-cavity search.

Pat-Down

During pat-down searches, corrections officers make quick visual and manual inspections of external body parts, clothing, bags and other personal effects.

Only outer garments, headgear (wigs or hats), footwear (socks and shoes), accessories (jewelry or bandages), and items in pockets are to be removed during a pat-down search. These can be checked for prohibited items in secret compartments, such as pocket linings and shoe soles/heels.

Clothed-Body

During clothed-body searches, corrections officers make longer, more thorough visual and manual inspections than they do pat-down searches. They may also check the oral (mouth), aural (ear), and nasal (nose) cavities, and make persons being searched run their fingers through the hair. Aside from the articles mentioned in pat-down search, prosthetic limbs and dentures must be removed during a clothed-body search.

Strip Search

During strip searches, corrections officers make thorough visual inspections of body surfaces and objects, as described in clothed-body searches. However, strip searches require the removal of clothing and jewelry. In strip searches, at least two officers of the same gender as the person being searched must be present.

Body-Cavity Search

During highly exhaustive body-cavity searches, corrections officers make through visual inspections of the same body parts and orifices as those checked in clothed-body and strip searches. Unless discouraged by higher authorities, body-cavity searches involve technology-aided inspections of the rectal cavity and vaginal cavity. In some cases, the inspection calls for an X-ray.

In other highly suspicious cases, the forced intake of laxatives may be necessary to expel swallowed substances from the digestive system through bowel movement. In body-cavity searches, at least two officers of the same gender as the person being searched, plus medical staff, must be present.

Seizures

Seizures complement searches, particularly when prohibited items or controlled substances are found in the process. These seized articles must be documented and reported accordingly, to be used as evidence in any ensuing investigation.

Materiel

Materiel describes a correctional facility's non-human resources or assets, such as equipment, apparatus, office and warehouse supplies, vehicles, and defense systems. These are employed and applied in performing corrections functions efficiently, and in maintaining safety and security effectively.

Facility personnel, not excluding corrections officers, will be held accountable for damaged, lost, abused, misused, or tampered materiel. Therefore, they must fully understand the procedures, goals, and restrictions in regard to the conscientious use and proper care of these assets.

Referring to manuals and technical guides, consulting with technicians, and/or reporting any observed malfunction to the department or section responsible for immediate repair or disposition, are related tasks in handling materiel.

The unethical use of equipment warrants administrative sanctions. An example would be bringing home a few sheets of bond paper and half a box of paper clips to be used at home. Another would be extracting data from official documents for personal gain, such as writing and selling fiction based on inmate records.

Lack of ethical considerations in handling facility materiel can also lead to crimes, such as pilfering food supplies and stealing information to abet an act of espionage. In this case, facility personnel who are caught guilty will be investigated and subjected to criminal proceedings.

Administrative materiel includes tables and chairs, telephones and fax machines, photocopiers and cameras, computer software and peripherals, appliances and office supplies.

Security materiel includes electronic monitoring equipment (eg, closed-circuit cameras and television) and mechanical alarms, lighting systems and auxiliary power supply, barriers and lock, inmate restraints and personnel defense systems.

Warehouse and general stores items include clothing and footwear, beddings and toiletries, and other non-consumables and consumables prescribed and permitted by law.

Other equipment and supplies include appliances in the kitchen, furniture across the facility, warehouse items like clothing and beddings, medical supplies, emergency devices like fire extinguishers, communication equipment like handheld radios, service vehicles, and alternate power sources like generators.

Force, Restraint and Defensive Tactics

Force

Although a contentious topic, the use of force is legally applicable as long as it is used to a reasonable extent, particularly in self-defense and in protecting innocent lives. Rules and regulations on the use of force may vary in minor ways, but the overall objective is the same.

The word *reasonable* qualifies the use of force, and draws the line between legal and illegal. It relates to *de minimis* use of force in restraining and subduing a subject. This is akin to a push, a shove, or an injury that is not discernible, serious, or life-threatening. Reasonable use of force means the responsible employment of authorized forms that will impede a dangerous person's ability to cause serious trouble. Under no circumstances can "use of force" be equated with punishment and brutality. Similarly, use of force should never be seen as a way to instill fear, harass, and/or terrorize.

In the context of incarceration, use of force is a last resort in dealing with an inmate whose actuation has become serious, realistic threats to life and property. In other words, where negotiation and the pacific settlement of volatile issues are no longer possible, corrections officers may be compelled to take forceful, forcible action.

Again, the aim is to impede criminal movements and incapacitate unmanageable, assaultive, combative inmates. This is only done briefly, until such time as the subjects are contained. In using reasonable force, there are different styles and approaches that include employing physical restraints of the inmates themselves, and/or deploying defense systems.

Before resorting to physical measures, the force applied consists of psychological tactics. Styles of this nature include:

- Isolation (putting inmates in solitary confinement)
- Presence (instilling fear in inmates by making figures of power, influence, or authority appear before them)
- Verbalization (commanding inmates to contain themselves and warning them of harsh consequences and stiff penalties)

Types of Physical Restraints

Physical restraints are not used for punishment. Rather, these are means of subduing hostile inmates who exhibit hostile behavior that threaten their own or other people's safety. There are several different types of physical restraints.

Pinion Restraints

These are contraptions bigger than mechanical restraints. Examples are restraint boards, restraint chairs, four-point restraints on a stretcher, and swaddling devices.

Mechanical Restraints

These are usually portable, non-electronic devices that restrict inmate movement, especially when they are walking or in transit. Examples are handcuffs, hobbles, leg irons, safety straps, spit masks, tethers, and waist chains.

Chemical Restraints

These are formulated to disorient unyielding and assaultive inmates in order to give corrections officers enough time to react and gain control of the situation. After use, corrections officers and medical staff must advise the subjects to wash their faces and other body surfaces that have been exposed to it. Pepper spray and tear gas are chemical restraints.

Electronic Restraints

These require the use of electricity, mostly from batteries, in order to be effective. Many jurisdictions, however, do not allow the use of any or all electronic restraints on the grounds that use of these devices is cruel and inhumane.

Examples of electronic restraints placed on the subjects include wireless handcuffs and stun belts attached to combative inmates, and which set off and jolt them when they attempt to free themselves from the restraints.

Examples of electronic restraints that thwart assaults from a distance include stun shields (commonly used in cell extractions), stun grenades (used in dispersing violent crowds), and stun "guns" (used in jolting fleeing subjects from as far as ten meters).

Other Non-Lethal Restraints

Examples include batons, rubber truncheons, rubber bullets, and K9 teams. Such restraints must be applied judiciously, and must not be akin to cruel and inhumane punishment. Incorrect application can permanently maim or, in worst-case scenarios, kill the persons being restrained.

Corrections officers must ensure that all physical restraints do not cause inmates undue discomfort or humiliation, inflict physical pain or damage on bodily organs, or restrict the flow of oxygen and blood. When employing physical restraints, they must log the steps taken, and undertake procedures in the presence of medical staff and/or authorized personnel.

Firearms

Firearms are the least desirable method and recourse in impeding the movement and/or incapacitating an extremely hostile subject. Although it is allowed by many states, firearms can lead to death of the subject or of others, and the circuitous and stressful investigations that follow. Firearms have their own protocols; an example would be shouting warnings like "Freeze!" and "Stop, or I'll shoot!"

Immediate Use of Force

This refers to an extremely urgent situation, in which delaying the use of force can escalate a volatile situation and result in damage to property, and injury or death of persons. An example would be a brawl between a few inmates that erupts into a prison-gang war. Another would be an inmate arguing irrationally with a corrections officer, then getting his possé to aid him in assaulting the latter.

Calculated Use of Force

This refers to a not-so-urgent situation that can be contained, but which calls for an inmate being physically restrained. Although there is no immediate threat to safety, the least amount of force is applied. For example an inmate may need to be extracted from a cell because he has sexually assaulted another inmate.

Excessive Use of Force

In corrections, this refers to the abusive, malicious, and sadistic manner of treating inmates, physically and psychologically. Because it violates an individual's constitutional rights, facility personnel who condone and/or engage in the unreasonable application of restraints can be held criminally and administratively liable.

One frequently discussed case, *Hudson v McMillian,* illustrates the consequences of the excessive use of force. In October 1983, Louisiana state penitentiary inmate Keith Hudson got in an altercation with corrections officer Jack McMillian. With colleagues Marvin Woods and Arthur Mezo, McMillian restrained Hudson with handcuffs and shackles, and led him to the lockdown area. Hudson sued the corrections officers, alleging that on the way to the lockdown area, McMillian punched him in the eyes, mouth, chest, and stomach as Woods held the inmate and kicked him from behind. Meanwhile Mezo, who was the supervisor on duty, did not exert any effort to stop the brutality, and only reminded his two colleagues "not to have too much fun". The inmate sustained bruises, loosened teeth, and a crack in his dental plate.

In 1991, the court sided with Hudson, having determined that the corrections officers' conduct was "objectively unreasonable because no force was required" in containing Hudson. It further stated that McMillian and Woods "qualified as clearly excessive and occasioned unnecessary and wanton infliction of pain."

Pre-Incident Review

In cases where there is an anticipated critical incident and a necessity for the calculated use of force, facility administrators and supervisors study and approve tactical plans. Upon engagement of the ground element/s, they observe and document situations, movements, responses, and maneuvers.

Post-Incident Review

After the dust has settled, even in situations that require the immediate use of force, the command group and mid-level managers review the entire incident, identify challenges and opportunities, draw lessons and good practices, and begin the interrogation and investigation processes.

Corrections officers directly involved are summoned for debriefing, and are most likely required to undergo critical incident stress management therapy. Facility staff and inmates who have witnessed, or who have been caught in the middle, are also encouraged to undergo therapy.

Defensive Tactics

Formally called empty-hand control measures (EHCM), the term *defensive tactics* refers to a system of manual techniques in applying force on—and subduing—assaultive inmates or other hostile subjects.

As with physical restraints, the goal of EHCM includes repelling threatening behavior, dispersing riots, and extracting hostages. Training in defensive tactics translates to arming corrections officers with confidence, advantage, and the actual capacity to tackle an assailant (or, quite possibly, a number of assailants).

The principles of defensive tactics underpin the following training objectives:

- Harnessing balance, body mechanics, and leverage

- Making strength overcome weakness

- Outmaneuvering attackers by exploiting their strength and momentum—even if they are armed

New-millennium course developers and instructors have evolved in approach, drawing techniques from different martial arts and combining these with contact sports like boxing and wrestling. However, the fundamentals of the past still hold.

In the 1950s the FBI (then under the directorship of J Edgar Hoover) released a video presentation on defensive tactics for law enforcers who "must stay alert to stay alive."

The underlying principles apply to today's corrections officers, who remain vulnerable to attacks but are not at all defenseless, given their physical fitness training standards. Speed and skill are critical: In a real-life encounter, there is no second chance.

In defensive tactics, personal weapons are the most valuable. These are parts of the body that wield the power to counterattack when used correctly. For example, the hand is not only potent when formed into a fist. The edge can be made to "chop", while the fingers can be made to jab. Outcomes include severe pain, loss of consciousness, or more crippling results.

The following body parts are personal weapons:

- Head
- Hand
- Elbow
- Knee
- Foot

Meanwhile, learning to identify the areas where the body is structurally weak gives two advantages – the ability to parry strikes and blows targeted to these parts, and the ability to counterattack by striking at these parts of the opponent, such as the temple, bridge of the nose, or solar plexus.

Team-Based Tactics

Cell Extraction

Cell extraction is the procedure by which an inmate is forcibly removed from his or her cell for a valid reason determined by facility authorities. In most instances, inmates are asked to step out of their respective quarters and submit themselves for investigation of an infraction. If they do not come out despite their supervisors' calm and respectful request, these inmates subject themselves to cell extraction.

As with any use-of-force modes, a cell extraction is not the disciplinary mechanism *per se*. Rather, it is the means by which uncooperative and unyielding inmates are taken out of "hiding", then made to present themselves to facility authorities.

There is no national standard that dictates cell-extraction policies, and each facility formulates its own. In any case, the procedures should be anchored on inmate rights. Otherwise, inmates can sue the facility for violating their right to fair treatment.

There have been many instances where an inmate has resisted the cell extraction team and caused bodily harm in the process, or in which members of the cell extraction team committed brutality against the subject inmate.

Organization

Selection of the team (usually three to five members) is made. The team leader is appointed, and members are given their exact positions within the formation, as well as responsibilities and equipment. The front element bears the stun shield that protects the team by jolting the subject in case of a belligerent reaction. In current practice, the rear element holds the video to document the procedure.

Team members have specific tasks, such as dispersing pepper spray and tackling the subject. Each team member has a designated limb to immobilize. For example, Team Members One and Two take one arm each as Team Members Three and Four take a leg each, and work together in strapping the subject to a stretcher.

Training

Cell extraction basics are taught, and the team members get acquainted with each other to strengthen their coordination. Part of the training emphasizes the reasonable use of reasonable force and what modes will be used for specific circumstances. The objective of the actual cell extraction is to overwhelm the stubborn subject within the shortest duration—given the tiny cell space and the anticipated violent resistance.

Planning

A tactical plan is drawn as soon as there is a need for cell extraction. The team will be briefed on the background of the subject, the violation for which s/he is needed to submit to the facility authorities, and how the cell extraction will be carried out.

Planning considerations include the cell type (single or shared with other inmates), number of subjects to be extracted, number of inmates in the cell from which subject will be extracted, and so forth.

Activation

At the command of superiors, the cell extraction team begins to execute the plan and marches to the cell of the subject. After a final call to "surrender" and submit peacefully, the team enters the cell and carries out the plan.

In enclosed cells, resisting inmates usually use their mattresses as a shield against the cell extraction team. In this case, pepper spray is used to disorient the subject and—quite literally—lower his defenses.

When the subject is tackled and restrained with mechanical or pinion devices (depending on the level of resistance exhibited even at this point), s/he will be turned over to the authorities that ordered the appearance.

Documentation

It is a good practice to record the actual unfolding of events in video, first and foremost. This not only helps improve procedures and the overall response time; recording events also comes in handy during any complaints lodged by the subject. It is not uncommon for subjects to subject the involved corrections officers to an adjudication process and declare that the cell extraction teams have violated their right to fair treatment. As with any facility procedure, the team (through the leader) is expected to sign and file a report in a timely and thorough manner.

Review

Debriefing and post-event assessment are two sub-processes in cell extraction.

Correctional Emergency Response Team (CERT)

The CERT is an incarceration facility's special operations group that executes emergency plans, particularly those involving violent incidents and disturbances of the peace within the institution.

Ideally, elements of a facility's CERT are highly trained, fully equipped, and unit-cohesive to minimize risks of unsuccessful operations. Some call them "commandos" who engage in close-quarters confrontation with hostile inmates, while others look up to them as members of the facility's élite squad. In any case, they are burdened with the responsibility of keeping the staff, uninvolved inmates, and the community safe and secure in the most dangerous scenarios.

There is neither a national standard nor a government regulating agency to oversee CERT. Like a cell extraction team, it is a specialized unit created within facility policy and, most importantly, in congruence with the law.

A routine job for CERTs is cell extraction and riot control. Mobilization may be ordered outside of the premises if the situation calls for it. Examples would be deploying the CERT in hot pursuit operations to pin down an escaping inmate, and sending out the CERT during high-risk transport.

The justification for maintaining such teams in the corrections setting is comparable to that of the Special Weapons and Tactics Team (or SWAT) in law enforcement. However, CERTs put more emphasis on the use of non-lethal weapons to overpower their subjects, although this does not mean that they are restricted from using firearms.

It is important to note that even with a CERT in place, other corrections officers must not be complacent. In a facility, all personnel are required to be vigilant and alert at all times, and knowledgeable of all procedures in dealing with emergency situations.

Emergencies

Emergency Preparedness

Emergency preparedness means having a full understanding of unforeseen, untoward incidents that can occur within an environment, and possessing the readiness to respond with urgency and efficiency. In the corrections setting, emergency preparedness requires more vigilance, better capacities, and a higher degree of readiness than usual. In fact, every facility must have an emergency response unit, and a set of emergency-specific plans that all personnel must thoroughly understand.

Critical Incident Response

While it is true that an incarceration facility is a normally volatile environment, with threats of violence outbreaks hovering over it every day, there are more emergency situations (or critical incidents) than the common disturbances that are anticipated.

In a critical incident, correctional authorities are responsible for the safety of the entire workforce and the inmate population. They must establish a plan to evacuate everyone efficiently and ensure that inmates will not use the emergency as a means to escape and—consequently—to jeopardize the security of the community.

The National Institute of Corrections has recommended that incarceration facilities across the United States devise a comprehensive emergency preparedness strategy, and design plans for every conceivable critical incident. Ideally, the plans involve the correctional institution's top brass, who will head the decision-making process. As necessary, these will also call for cooperation with outside agencies like the FBI or local law enforcers, and other support services.

Emergency preparedness plans also institute a system that involves protocols and procedures, ad hoc command structures that will oversee tactical operations, specially trained and equipped response teams, alternate courses of action and worst-case scenarios, authority and limitations on the use of force, schedules of drills and simulations, and so forth.

Although critical incidents are usually of a violent nature that lead to a lockdown, general emergencies may include "non-violent" situations like equipment malfunction or the outbreak of a serious, infectious disease. Even in these cases, corrections officers are required to report the occurrence of a critical incident or crisis situation to the designated departments within the organization. Again, failure to do so may result in dire consequences.

In crisis situations, procedures usually involve the following:

- Logging details on how notification has been received
- Activating facility alert mechanisms

  (radio, telephone, pull boxes, panic alarm system)
- Contacting emergency response teams
- Alerting superiors and colleagues
- Administering first aid and/or CPR when necessary
- Conducting search and retrieval
- Evacuating staff and inmates
- Filing reports and writing assessments

Examples of general emergencies include:

- Work stoppage and/or walkout
- Food/hunger strike
- Battery of staff
- Inmate sexual assault on an employee or another inmate
- Inmate brawl or riot
- Inmate escape
- Hostage situation
- Bomb threat
- Fire/natural disaster/hazardous material.

High-Level Critical Situations

Inmate Escape

As soon as an inmate escape is reported, corrections officers are alerted to perform such immediate tasks as accounting for their respective units, containing and securing those who are not part of the escape, and joining in pursuit operations as ordered.

Hostage Situation

Surprisingly, many inmates who perpetrate hostage situations do so not because they want to be released from incarceration, but because they want to air their grievances. They feel maltreated by prison staff, including corrections officers, and think the only way to correct the system is forcing the authorities, the media, and/or the community to heed their requests for fairer and more humane treatment.

When a hostage situation takes place, negotiations follow. These are carried out by a team of individuals who have been trained to resolve and manage issues under extreme pressure. The objectives in negotiation involve "softening" the criminal behavior of the hostage-taker/s, persuading them to settle in a more amicable way, rescuing the hostages, and minimizing the casualty rate.

The fundamental process in wrestling the advantage from the hostage-taker/s involve listening proactively and showing empathy, and recommending peaceful solutions without necessarily giving in to the demands. A facility must have the tactical capacity for rescuing hostages and—should the situation—escalate, for tackling the hostage-taker/s without further imperiling the hostage/s.

A corrections officer is prone to being taken hostage because of his or her frequent, direct contact with inmates. This is why extreme care must be taken at all times when dealing with the wards. If taken hostage, it is important for the corrections officer to remain calm and composed, and to be prepared for hours of waiting for release. There is no justification in patronizing the hostage-takers or addressing them in an arrogant, threatening manner.

Bomb Threat

A bomb threat may or may not have substance. However, it is not for facility administrators and staff to dismiss as a hoax without properly evaluating the circumstances and letting experts search the surroundings.

The individual who receives the bomb threat writes down the message and all other information available. If the bomb threat is made by telephone, the following details are necessary: caller identity (any given name or alias, number of the phone used, voice characteristics, accent, other leads like sounds in the background), time of call, supposed location and detonation schedule of the bomb, declared reason for planting the bomb and/or demands.

Basic procedures during a bomb threat include alerting personnel and ordering a search of their immediate work areas for suspicious materials. Corrections officers will look around their designated units for the same, and report any anomalous or extraordinary object to their superiors.

A correctional institution with a bomb plan in place normally deploys its K9 unit, composed of bomb-sniffing dogs and their handlers, to search the premises for suspicious materials. Bomb technicians are also deployed to remove and/or disarm any bombs or improvised explosive devices (or IEDs).

Fire/Natural Disaster/Hazardous Material

Owing to national requirements, correctional facilities have emergency preparedness plans with respect to fire, its different classes and the types of fire extinguishers to be used for each class. However, not all institutions are ready for a *force majeure* - a natural disaster like an earthquake or a super storm.

Moreover, only a few have full capabilities and updated training of efficient responses, such as mass evacuations, during critical incidents where hazardous material (HAZMAT) is involved. An example of a HAZMAT-related emergency would be a chemical spill and release in the vicinity.

Evacuating Inmates

Corrections officers are trained on the facility's evacuation plan for any type of crisis situation that requires moving people out of their normal posts. Their duties are primarily to transfer inmates to safer ground within the facility or to an off-site holding area. Evacuating disabled persons is difficult enough, but evacuating physically or mentally handicapped inmates can get a lot more challenging. There are two million such individuals incarcerated in prisons and jails across the United States. Their evacuation in case of emergency must be compliant with the Americans with Disabilities Act of 1990.

First Aid/CPR/AED

Corrections officers are trained to administer basic treatment or relief on individuals in need of urgent medical attention. While waiting for the facility's emergency response team, or the local emergency medical service (or EMS) to arrive, they must be able to apply first aid and/or cardiopulmonary resuscitation (CPR), and use the automated external defibrillator (AED) whenever necessary. Using disposable gloves and other protective devices (like masks) is recommended when providing medical treatment.

First Aid

First aid is the set of life-saving techniques given to an injured or ill person if trained medical providers are not immediately available. In the corrections setting, techniques may come in handy for such situations as:

- Burns
- Drowning
- Choking
- Poisoning
- Head, neck, or spine injuries

- External bleeding
- Falling unconscious
- Stroke
- Heart attack

Cardiopulmonary Resuscitation

Abbreviated as CPR, this technique is applied when the person is suspected of cardiac arrest, which must not be mistaken for a heart attack. If not addressed immediately, within ten minutes, a person suffering from cardiac arrest could die. The aim of CPR is to restore blood circulation that has ceased during an episode of cardiac arrest.

Based on updated national CPR guidelines, the order of interventions on inmates should be chest compressions first, then airway, before the procedure on breathing.

Automated External Defibrillator

Abbreviated as AED, the automated external defibrillator is a portable machine that can diagnose life-threatening cardiac conditions. The portable electronic device, which should be available in all correctional facilities, is also designed to treat said conditions through defibrillation and immediately restore the patient's "heart rhythm" to normalcy.

The AED is designed for layperson use. With proper training, corrections officers can use it to provide immediate treatment to inmates, staff, and other persons in the facility.

Supervision, Discipline and Transport

Supervision

Corrections officers provide inmates care and maintenance while in their custody and control. In order to be effective and successful in their mission, they must know inmates' rights and responsibilities by heart. Otherwise, corrections officers can be held in violation of the law. Despite their debt to society, inmates are entitled to certain constitutional guarantees:

Right to Equal Protection

Under the Fourteenth Amendment, inmates cannot be discriminated on the basis of race, gender, sexual orientation, religion, or political belief. The only exception of segregation based on this is when security of the facility is compromised. For example, aggressive neo-Nazis, especially those who have committed hate crimes, will not be housed with Jews to avoid violence. Conversely, no inmate can pay corrections authorities to get preferential treatment.

Right to Fair Treatment

Under the Eighth Amendment, inmates cannot be subject to cruel, inhumane, and disrespectful treatment. As earlier discussed, even extremely hostile wards cannot be slapped with physical or psychological punishments, and restraining them should only be done to keep them from harming others or damaging property.

Right to Due Process

Under the Fifth and Fourteenth Amendments, inmates cannot be sanctioned without being investigated and submitted to proper procedures. They are entitled to lodge administrative appeals. Similarly, they have the right to be notified of the violations for which they are being investigated, and the right to a legal counsel.

Right to Privacy

Under the Fourth Amendment, inmates enjoy a limited right to privacy. Although pat-downs and clothed-body searches are basic in maintaining safety and security within the facility, probable cause must be established to pursue strip searches or body-cavity searches. In such situations, procedures will have to be followed.

Other rights include:

- Right to be informed of facility policies and procedures
- Right to healthcare
- Right to practice religion or any form of worship
- Right to participate in educational activities
- Right to participate in employment training
- Right to be heard

Inmates who are terminally ill or who have physical disabilities, as well as female inmates who are pregnant, have rights to specialized healthcare. Their conditions exempt them from being shackled, among others. Normally, women who give birth in prison may be eligible for house arrest, to ensure that their newborn children do not get exposed to harsh jail or prison conditions.

Bivens Action

Bivens action (or Bivens complaint) refers to a lawsuit that can be filed against any federal or state official and agent, including corrections personnel, whose discharge of official duties are thought to be in violation of constitutional rights of persons. The action is particularly meant to obtain monetary relief.

Deliberate Indifference

Deliberate indifference refers to intentionally neglecting the duty of preserving the peace in the facility, and protecting inmates from harm. Corrections officers who exhibit deliberate indifference are culpable of violating inmate guarantees under the Eighth Amendment, particularly the right to fair treatment and the implied freedom to exist without fear of being subject to the cruelty of others.

One frequently discussed case, *Farmer v Brennan, et al*, illustrates the consequences of deliberate indifference. Dee Farmer, a born-male transgender person exhibiting feminine characteristics, was a federal prisoner sentenced in the mid-1980s to 20 years for credit card fraud (a non-violent crime). At a point in his incarceration, he was transferred to what was then the Terre Haute USP.

Despite being segregated for safety reasons in the previous prisons, Farmer was placed with the general male population at said maximum-security penitentiary. There, he would be mauled and raped by inmates, one of whom Farmer had even accused of infecting him with HIV.

In a Bivens complaint, Farmer sued Edward Brennan, in his official capacity as the warden of the Terre Haute USP, and several other respondents within the corrections system. The action alleged that the prison officials denied him the Eight Amendment right to fair treatment. He sought compensatory and punitive damages, and an injunction that would ensure his non-confinement in any such facility as the Terre Haute USP. The Supreme Court ultimately ruled in favor of Farmer, having noted the conscious disregard of a potentially significant risk that an inmate can suffer during incarceration. Thus, it held the respondents liable for deliberate indifference.

It is society's duty to protect the life, health, and dignity of inmates, and it is the corrections system's responsibility to carry out that duty efficiently.

Grievance Procedure

Grievance procedure refers to the system through which inmates can file complaints about their conditions inside the facility. Their issues are addressed by an inspector, an impartial party assigned by the regulatory body of a particular jurisdiction (such as federal and state) to watch over prison and jail operations.

Inmates are encouraged to discuss their concerns with facility administrators first, before lodging the complaint. However, if they are not satisfied with the outcome, inmates can fill out and submit the form accordingly. Usual grievances are derelict facility conditions and abusive behavior of facility staff.

The grievance procedure is confidential in nature, and guarantees inmates protection from reprisals. No corrections officer or facility personnel named in the complaint form can treat the complainant negatively in retribution.

Consistent with the inmates' rights described above, corrections officers must ensure that inmates have access to the following:

- Hygiene and personal grooming

- Sanitary conditions

- Information, such as library materials

- Correspondence on legal and family matters

- Counseling (on stress management, family relationships, other)

- Accounted-for personal funds for commissary and other purchases

- In-facility employment (where available)

- Grievance system

- Mail

- Visitation

- Nutritious meals

However, some inmates are stripped of rights even after they have served their sentences and released from incarceration. As earlier discussed, those who have been found guilty of felonies suffer from legal stigmatization. Thus, they are not allowed to exercise rights like vote and serve on a jury. This condition can only be reversed by the jurisdiction that has charged and sentenced them.

Additionally, inmates are not allowed to profit from their criminal experiences under the Son of Sam law. Neither are their families, fiduciaries or friends allowed to profit from the story. If proven that they have violated the Son of Sam law, any gains may be awarded by the court to the victims' families or the US Treasury.

Discipline

With inmates' rights come responsibilities. Basic inmate obligations include treating facility staff, fellow inmates, and other people with respect; and strictly observing facility rules and regulations. Committing prohibited acts and/or infractions is tantamount to disciplinary sanctions.

Corrections officers prepare a disciplinary report on any infraction or violation to the department concerned. In turn, facility administrators will determine the gravity or severity of the violation, and the applicable sanction. Again, there is a process for punishing offenders, and disciplinary hearings take place because inmates have the right to due process.

Disciplinary and administrative sanctions depend on the severity of the violation. From the most severe to the least, the following are disciplinary sanctions available in most correctional facilities:

- Rescission or retardation of parole date (if applicable)
- Forfeiture or withholding of good conduct time credit (up to 100%)
- Termination or disallowance of good conduct time
- Disciplinary segregation (up to one year)
- Monetary restitution and/or fine
- Loss of privileges (telephone, recreation, other)
- Removal from programs and activities
- Extra duty

Corporal punishment is forbidden under any circumstances. It is important to emphasize that physical force applied to an inmate is only for restrictive purposes, which are geared toward suppressing potential outbreaks of violence.

Disciplinary Hearing

A disciplinary hearing is part of the proceedings that determine whether or not an inmate is innocent of an infraction. Like court, a disciplinary hearing examines the circumstances reported against an inmate and what sanction will be dispensed for violation of rules. Sanctions are not arbitrary, and must be within guidelines.

The conduct of disciplinary proceedings must uphold the inmate's right to due process, the right to deny the charge/s and defend oneself, and the right to appeal the decision.

Investigation

Before the hearing proper, an investigation takes place. If the infraction is administrative in nature, it will be pursued by the internal administrative investigation unit. If it is criminal in nature, it will be pursued by the internal criminal investigation unit. Investigations assume law enforcement functions, and are undertaken on the grounds that policy stipulations have been breached. Witnesses are normally involved, and they can be corrections officers, other facility personnel, inmates, or outside persons who may have been present at the time of the violation.

Examples of cases that are commonly investigated include:

- Security breaches
- Gang activities
- Assaults (aggravated, simple, or sexual)
- Narcotic smuggling and use
- Fraternization between staff and inmates (where involved staff will be investigated as well)

Transport

Corrections officers often escort inmates to and from the facility, especially on court summons or when inmates need to be transferred to an offsite medical facility. In transporting inmates, they must have a full grasp of security and control procedures, as outlined and detailed in the facility policy. These procedures include the proper and humane use of restraints, such as handcuffs and leg weights, inside the vehicle and at the destination point.

Corrections officers are also expected to learn safety procedures to protect themselves, their colleagues, and other persons from inmate resistance, ambush, and even road accidents that can undermine the security of the transport party. Aspects of inmate transport include:

- Mass movement
- High-risk transport (where security measures are tighter)
- Ground, air, water transport
- International/cross-border transport

- Medical transport (where knowledge of medical care may be necessary).

Mental Health Issues

Involuntary Commitment

Also referred to as involuntary admission or call emergency, involuntary commitment in the corrections setting relates to the necessity of an inmate to be submitted to treatment when s/he begins to show symptoms of an acute mental illness or psychiatric disorder. The term *involuntary* is descriptive of an inmate's perceived reaction to said commitment, but it does not imply a forcible act on the part of corrections officers.

Involuntary commitment is supported by a court order. However, it is only legal if the inmate who is up for commitment has shown inarguable signs of endangering oneself or others. Evidence of this must be presented. The Florida Mental Health Act of 1971, otherwise known as the Baker Act, allows examining and institutionalizing inmates in that mental state.

Counseling Inmates

Part of a corrections officer's duty is to give good counsel to inmates, especially in resolving personal issues. This is to promote peaceable and calm conditions in the facility, and goodwill in general.

Inmates are under stressful conditions, and not only because of their environment. Their anxieties also originate from within themselves because of factors like guilt, shame, self-depreciation, hopelessness, and unpleasant news about their spouses and other family members.

Because of these internal troubles, inmates are at a very high risk of suicide or, at the very least, self-injury. Sadly, suicide is the leading cause of inmate death, next only to illnesses, but far more than homicide, substance overdose (drug/alcohol intoxication), and accidental death combined. In 2011 alone, there were 495 inmates from local jails and state prisons who died by suicide, most commonly by hanging.

In order to prevent the epidemic, corrections officers must be able to detect indicators that an inmate is contemplating suicide. A telltale sign is when an inmate floats the idea of suicide, even if said jokingly. Another is when an inmate shows extreme restlessness or mood swings. There are cases when suicidal inmates distribute their personal belongings to friends shortly before making their attempt; events such as these must be taken into consideration for heightened monitoring.

When corrections officers see the possibility of a suicide, their immediate response must be to offer the prisoner a listening ear, encouragement, and empathy. The next urgent steps should involve removing objects that can be used to execute the suicide, and alerting supervisors in order for them to send mental health professionals to the inmates-in-question.

Stress Management for Corrections Officers

For all their service to society and to the inmates themselves, corrections officers are vulnerable to stress, which is harmful and destructive when not managed properly. Stress—along with burnout and demoralization—is not only from the volatile situation of inmates. It is also caused by organizational problems like low budgets, ineffective administration, office politics, corrupt practices, and other factors.

Although there are programs formulated to address the issue, corrections officers must also learn how to cope with stress on their own. Stress-management techniques include:

- Desensitization
- Relaxation
- Meditation
- Communication
- Problem-solving

When mastered, these techniques will not only relieve stress in a temporary sense. It will also help corrections officers overcome emotional and mental fatigue on the long term, and enable them to experience job appreciation and satisfaction. Taken as a whole, resolving stress issues will positively impact the performance of the facility, the corrections field, and the entire criminal justice system.

Becoming a Supervisor

Leadership skills, efficiency in the discharge of functions, and the ability to maintain professional relationships (with personnel, inmates, and other individuals) determine a correction officer's eligibility for higher responsibilities.

When corrections officers are elevated as supervisors, they do not forget the basic roles: processing and supervising inmates, reporting to immediate supervisors, responding to emergencies, and making sure that the facility is up to standards and in compliance with the law. Rather, they sharpen their capacities in these areas because they will be given bigger units to monitor, maintain, and optimize. This expansion in the job description includes overseeing other corrections officers and their respective unit assignments, among others.

Supervisory duties include:

- Planning and directing operations in their assigned units

- Training and motivating subordinates

- Ensuring the smooth flow of work between operations and administration

- Making swift, solid decisions on matters concerning their units

- Managing and resolving conflict

- Solving as many problems at their level as their position allows

- Reporting to the next higher level in the facility hierarchy

Promotion to the position of corrections supervisor often requires a bachelor's degree, advanced training in corrections administration and operations, and a certain level of actual experience as an entry-level corrections officer.

Sample Test Items

The following culminates the series of mini-practice tests during your CCO exam review. This part focuses on reading comprehension, and it also tests your ability to follow instructions.

1. **To what privileges are female and above-40 corrections officers generally entitled?**

   a. administrative and clerical duties

   b. exemption from violent environments

   c. morning shifts and extended lunch periods

   d. none of the above

   Correct answer: D. Choice D is correct; female and above-40 corrections officers are not typically excused from areas of assignment, including dangerous duty detail.

2. **What is the primary purpose of the corrections officer code of ethics and professional conduct?**

   a. discipline and professionalism

   b. documentation and records management

   c. promotion and career advancement

   d. welfare and morale

   Correct answer: A. Choice A is correct; codes of ethics and conduct are formulated to regulate the behavior of corrections officers.

3. **What clearly violates strip-search procedures?**

   a. manual inspection of items from coat pockets

   b. visual inspection of the naked body

   c. checking of artificial limbs and/or dentures

   d. conduct by one corrections officer

Correct answer: D. Choice D is correct; a one-person inspection of an individual during strip search is against the rules.

4. **In what situation would a female corrections officer be exempted from personal liability and/or granted immunity?**

   a. She punched the nose of a non-aggressive male visitor, who happened to be the husband of the inmate who started the violent altercation with another inmate at the lobby.

   b. She visited the diarrhea-stricken Chinese inmate at the dispensary after refusing to serve the latter potable water that she said was meant for white inmates.

   c. She failed to revive the chaplain because the emergency medical equipment malfunctioned.

   d. She feared for her life, so she kept quiet about her peers prostituting themselves to inmates.

Correct answer: C. Choice C is correct; it is the only humane and legal action among the choices.

5. **What procedure complements a search of the person?**

   a. X-ray

   b. seizure

   c. convulsions

   d. anesthesia

Correct answer: B. Choice B is correct; seizure of prohibited items or controlled substances is associated with—or, at times, a direct result of—a search.

6. **What must a corrections officer do when a pressing issue arises in his unit, but policy says that it is not for him to resolve this?**

   a.   engage the media and other community stakeholders in a referendum

   b.   ask a colleague and the chief of social workers to accompany him to the director

   c.   elevate the matter to his superior, but discuss it alongside justified recommendations

   d.   contact higher authorities the way he always does, even in petty situations

Correct answer: C. Choice C is correct; all other answers are absurd.

7. **Which attribute can be a core value in corrections?**

   a.   valor

   b.   animosity

   c.   litigation

   d.   oxymoron

Correct answer: A. Choice A is correct; all other choices do not belong to ideal value systems.

8. **Which phrase best describes unethical behavior in corrections?**

   a.   must be criminal in nature

   b.   automatically warrants court proceedings

   c.   refers to lack of either grooming habits or leadership skills

   d.   pertains to repulsive professional practices

Correct answer: D. Choice D is correct; unethical behavior is synonymous with repulsive, immoral practices in carrying out duties in corrections.

9. **Which statement best describes involuntary admission?**

    a.   Inmates are forced to go to prison.

    b.   Inmates are submitted for treatment of mental illnesses.

    c.   Inmates are compelled to confess their sins to the chaplain.

    d.   Inmates are coerced into to reveal confidential information.

Correct answer: B. Choice B is correct; mentally ill inmates do not necessarily agree that they need to be taken to the hospital for treatment.

10. **What factor could not have logically contributed to the escape of an inmate in a metal restraining device?**

    a. corrosion

    b. broken lock

    c. officer negligence

    d. voodoo incantation

Correct answer: D. Choice D is correct; under normal circumstances, supernatural reasons for escapes are not logical and valid.

11. **Which statement best describes procedures?**

    a. step-by-step direction of sub-processes to complete an action

    b. item-by-item list of materials needed to attain a target

    c. fact-by-fact narration of an event

    d. case-by-case analysis of an inmate incident

Correct answer: A. Choice A is correct; step-by-step direction or formula of what to do for a particular process, in a specific event, as with booking an inmate or carrying out a fire drill.

12. **Which phrase best describes the situation wherein a corrections officer chooses not to seek help for a bleeding inmate who started the riot that caused the injury?**

    a. deliberate indifference

    b. disciplinary disallowance

    c. institutional privilege

    d. qualified liability

Correct answer: A. Choice A is correct; deliberate indifference is intentional inaction to address issues, such as providing medical and humanitarian services even to problematic inmates.

13. **What is a situation where force should never be applied?**

    a. overcoming inmate resistance

    b. negating inmate hostility

    c. instilling inmate discipline

    d. repelling inmate aggression

Correct answer: C. Choice C is correct; force is not a disciplinary measure.

14. **Which phrase describes unreasonable use of force?**

    a. repelling an aggressive subject with a shield

    b. putting an assaultive female in isolation

    c. hog-tying a violent inmate with a nylon strap

    d. handcuffing a combative septuagenarian inmate

Correct answer: C. Choice C is correct; hog-tying not only causes humiliation but can also result in restricted blood flow, which makes it unreasonable, illegal, and punishable by law.

15. **What is not likely to happen to the corrections officer from a standards-compliant prison, who guns down two extremely hostile inmates acting in cahoots?**

    a. award-giving ceremony for bravery

    b. exemption from any debriefing or investigation

    c. questioning by administrators

    d. sense of relief that the situation has been contained

Correct answer: B. Choice B is correct; any critical incident, especially a grave one like this, is investigated and given proper closure.

16. **What is the most common reason for inmates to perpetrate hostage situations?**

    a. to sell their story to Hollywood

    b. to get their sentences cut short

    c. to obtain clemency

    d. to air unattended grievances

Correct answer: D. Choice D is correct; inmates who resort to hostage-taking situations declare that they are aggrieved by prison staff and that they are being routinely terrorized by authorities in the facility.

17. **What disciplinary sanction is prohibited?**

    a. forfeiture of good conduct time credit

    b. strapping to pinion restraints

    c. assigning extra duties in the kitchen

    d. charging fines

Correct answer: B. Choice B is correct; any form of restraint cannot be used in punishments and disciplinary sanctions.

18. **What right remains lost even if inmates have been released from incarceration?**

    a. right to remain silent

    b. right to the counsel of female criminal defense attorneys

    c. right to write a book about their criminal and prison experiences

    d. right to worship a Greek god and a Catholic icon at once

Correct answer: C. Choice C is correct; under the Son of Sam law, previously incarcerated persons cannot profit from, or enrich themselves by, making commercial products (eg, books and movies) out of their criminal life.

19. **What describes a released inmate's condition of not being allowed to vote or serve on a jury?**

    a. legal stigmatization

    b. disciplinary segregation

    c. involuntary commitment

    d. human rights violation

Correct answer: A. Choice A is correct; legal stigmatization, which includes disenfranchisement, is a consequence of imprisonment.

20. **What exemplifies *de minimis* use of force?**

    a. Officers order an inmate to face down when he scream vulgarities, and is suffocated with a pillow.

    b. Officers push an inmate to the wall of the cell after he attempts to whack them with his mattress-shield.

    c. Officers slap an inmate's nape with a roll of newspaper after he has beaten another inmate black and blue.

    d. Officers stun an inmate with a shield when he accidentally breaks a plate during kitchen duties.

Correct answer: B. Choice B is correct; pushing and shoving may be necessary to restrain an inmate who exhibits resistance, although these can be cruel and inhumane if applied to intimidate and punish.

21. Which phrase best describes the situation wherein a corrections officer chooses not to seek help for a bleeding inmate who started a riot?

   a. deliberate indifference

   b. disciplinary disallowance

   c. institutional privilege

   d. qualified liability

Correct answer: A. Choice A is correct; deliberate indifference is the intentional inaction to address issues, such as providing medical and humanitarian services even to problematic inmates.

22. What is not a common stress factor among corrections officers?

   a. office politics

   b. inmate violence

   c. corrupt administration

   d. desensitized environment

Correct answer: D. Choice D is correct; Choice D is correct; the phrase is ridiculous.

23. In which instance can low organizational budget be demotivating?

   a.   Deteriorated cell locks cannot be immediately replaced, which weakens security systems.

   b.   Inmates cannot be rewarded with fancy desserts, which are proven to be effective in rehabilitative diet.

   c.   Paid staff vacations abroad will not materialize, even if these are part of the basic remuneration package.

   d.   Construction of stone mosques and churches will be deferred until the next fiscal period.

Correct answer: A. Choice A is correct; weak security systems is a stressor and demotivator, especially for corrections officers.

Sample Observational Skills Test

Instructions

1. Use a stopwatch – you have ten minutes for this exercise.

2. Observe the scene in the painting.

3. Absorb as many details as you can.

4. When the time is up, go to the next page.

5. Answer each question without returning to this page.

6. Be honest. Remember: <u>Integrity is the foundation of America's CCOs.</u>

Scene at the Signing of the Constitution of the United States, *a 1940 oil-on-canvas painting by Howard Chandler Christy. Public-domain image.*

1. **Around what time of day is the scene taking place?**

    a. 12:00 a.m.

    b. 12:00 p.m.

    c. 10:00 p.m.

    d. There is no indication of time.

2. **Approximately how many persons are in the hall?**

    a. four score

    b. half a dozen

    c. three dozen

    d. over a hundred

3. **How many females are on the platform?**

    a. 0

    b. 1

    c. 2

    d. 3

4. **What is a possible reason for some people at the back to be extending their arms toward the platform?**

    a. They are impassioned, which is why they are pointing their swords.

    b. They are hostile, which is why they are pointing their guns at the platform.

    c. They are excited, which is why they are trying to raise a point.

    d. No one from the back is extending an arm at all.

5. **What can be seen on the wall to the right of the person in the middle of the platform?**

    a. calligraphic graffiti

    b. flags on staffs

    c. watercolor paintings

    d. windows with drapes

6. **With what is the platform almost covered?**

    a. human blood

    b. red carpet

    c. travertine stone

    d. injured soldiers

Answer Key:

    1. B

    2. C

    3. A

    4. C

    5. D

    6. B

Practice Test

Overview

This test has a total of 150 multiple-choice questions (MCQs) across the three areas: General Knowledge, Career Skills, and Understanding the Corrections System. The answer key is found at the end of the test. Some of the items found here may not have been discussed in the preceding study guide – it's your job to look them up!

I   **General Knowledge (80 items)**

     A.   Mathematics (15)

     B.   Terms and Concepts (25)

     C.   Grammar (15)

     D.   Reading Comprehension (25)

II   **Career Skills (20 items)**

     A.   Communication and Interpersonal Skills (5)

     B.   Administrative Skills (5)

     C.   Situational Reasoning (5)

     D.   Observational Skills (5)

III   **Understanding the Corrections System (50 items)**

General Knowledge

There are 80 MCQs across these sub-areas: Mathematics, Terms and Concepts, Grammar, and Reading Comprehension.

Mathematics

1. Suppose the annual budget for state prisons totals $57 billion, and the operating costs exceed it by 12.21 per cent; how much is actually spent in a year?

    a. $44,790,000,000

    b. $50,040,300,000

    c. $63,959,700,000

    d. $63,959,700,000

2. Suppose the taxpayer spends $57 billion annually to sustain state prisons with a total inmate population of 1,554,603. What is the inmate per-capita cost per year?

    a. $36,665.31

    b. $37,665.31

    c. $37,665.31

    d. $39,665.31

3. If one out of 100 American adults has been jailed at some point in his/her life, about how many among 240,144,241 American adults have experienced life behind bars?

    a. 240,144

    b. 2,401,443

    c. 24,014,430

    d. none of the above

4. In a facility, 89% of 720 inmates say they are willing to be disciplined according to applicable laws, policies, and standing procedures. About how many are against being corrected under the current program?

    a. 80
    b. 89
    c. 631
    d. 640

5. To prepare themselves for release, 212 inmates have decided to take one vocational class each. Half a dozen are into carpentry, a dozen into furniture repair, two dozen into automotive, and 3 ¾ dozen into food service. How many are studying another subject?

    a. 21
    b. 87
    c. 125
    d. 206

6. How many inmates are needed to finish washing 600 dishes in an hour if it takes three inmates to wash five dishes within a minute?

    a. 3
    b. 4
    c. 5
    d. 6

7. Six inmates can sort 1,221 laundry items in one and a half hours. What is the average number of laundry items that an inmate can sort in five minutes?

    a. 2.26
    b. 3.39
    c. 11.30
    d. 67.83

8. A cell block has 236 inmates, 186 of whom are checked out to the recreational program. Of those required to remain in the cell block, 11 were called for cleanup work in a separate building. How many did not actually leave the cell block?

   a. 11
   b. 39
   c. 46
   d. 50

9. How many minutes does it take to escort an inmate to trial and back using the same route, if the distance between the facility and the court is 13.5 miles, and the transport vehicle runs without any delays at 55 mph?

   a. 26.55
   b. 29.45
   c. 55.13
   d. 56.75

10. Prison Facility XYZ can accommodate up to 612 inmates. If the current population is 507, what is the occupancy rate?

   a. 15.17%
   b. 17.15%
   c. 82.84%
   d. 88.84%

11. **For maintaining good behavior and even with no chance at parole, Federal Inmate Robles can get his sentence reduced by up to 54 days per year of incarceration. If he is to serve a 25-year sentence with a clean record, on what year of his incarceration will he be eligible for release?**

    a. sixth

    b. eleventh

    c. sixteenth

    d. twenty-first

12. **There are 45 inmates in a group. One-fifth of them are convicted of white-collar crimes; one-third, drug-related felonies. How many are convicted of something else?**

    a. 12

    b. 21

    c. 33

    d. 42

13. **Prison Facility JKL is due to begin its program of training guide dogs for the blind. If it takes four inmates 70 hours to teach one dog a full course, how many inmates will be needed to train a dozen dogs completely in 245 hours?**

    a. 0

    b. 16.8

    c. 168

    d. 1,680

14. According to a 2011 report released by the United States Bureau of Labor Statistics, corrections officers earned an average of $43,300 annually. If there were 52 workweeks that year, about how much did they typically make for a fortnight's worth of duty?

    a. $833

    b. $1,665

    c. $3,331

    d. depends on the type of facility

15. According to the same report mentioned in Item 14, there were 424,300 correctional officers employed in facilities at the federal, state, local levels. If 59% were state prison guards and 3.8% were federal prison guards, how many served at the local level?

    a. 157,340

    b. 234,213

    c. 250,337

    d. 408,177

Terms and Concepts

16. **How does criminal justice define recidivism?**

    a. a corrections officer's acceptance of bribe from prisoners

    b. a corrections officer's own incarceration for assisting a former offender to crime

    c. a former offender's act of bribing a corrections officer

    d. a former offender's relapse into criminal activity and habits

17. **What best describes an incarcerated person?**

    a. an individual who is either sentenced to imprisonment or awaiting trial

    b. a juvenile who has successfully graduated from youth rehabilitation programs

    c. a female suspect who is pregnant upon arrest

    d. an offender whom federal agents are hunting down

18. **What best describes the corrections system in the United States?**

    a. It was built upon Abraham Lincoln's Gettysburg Address to help restore democracy in North America.

    b. It was forced upon the Native Americans as a result of the British invasion in the 1700s.

    c. It is an institution for punishing criminals and supervising their rehabilitation, release, and reintegration into society.

    d. It is an establishment that addresses gang wars.

19. **What falsity might Officer X have exhibited to be found guilty of perjury?**

    a. accusation that Inmate Q committed wrongdoing

    b. testimony under oath

    c. representation before the media as facility director

    d. affixed signature above an inmate's printed name

20. **What activity may be allowed for an inmate to engage in sexual intercourse with the legal spouse, to help preserve the marital bond?**

    a. peer counseling

    b. in-vitro fertilization

    c. family outing

    d. conjugal visit

21. What pertains to the maximum time that legal proceedings on a particular event can be initiated?

    a. statutory rights

    b. statute of limitations

    c. either a or b

    d. neither a nor b

22. In what situation is a person automatically guilty of a felony?

    a. He engages in a jewelry-store robbery that the owner has orchestrated to collect insurance.

    b. He is caught driving drunk.

    c. He exposes himself in a public place, including the Internet.

    d. He threatens to harm the people who are attending the funeral of a soldier killed in Afghanistan.

23. Prison guards assigned to maximum-security buildings will least likely deal with persons convicted of _____ .

    a. armed robbery

    b. parricide

    c. treason

    d. wire fraud

24. A prison is where an individual goes after _____ .

    a. shock therapy

    b. being sentenced to incarceration

    c. the jury finds his spouse innocent

    d. failing the training required in witness protection programs

25. A person can be accused of trafficking drugs if s/he is caught _____ .

    a. with a cigarette-sized stick of marijuana

    b. consuming heroin in the car

    c. manufacturing methamphetamine

    d. doing all of the above

26. "You have the right to remain silent," is part of a law enforcer's declaration that is commonly known as _____ ?

    a. Monroe Doctrine

    b. Miranda Warning

    c. Geneva Protocol

    d. Hippocratic Oath

27. A wealthy person's act of deliberately filing fraudulent tax returns is an example of _____ .

    a. an excusable act of negligence

    b. an improbable cause

    c. a blue-collar crime

    d. a white-collar crime

28. A law enforcer can be charged with unlawful detention _____ .

    a. when s/he lacks sufficient cause in detaining a person

    b. when s/he lacks sufficient evidence in detaining a person

    c. both A and B

    d. none of the above

29. The legal action that requires an arrested person to be presented before the court or brought before a judge, and which confirms whether or not the prisoner has been legally detained, is called _____ .

    a. writ of amparo

    b. writ of certiorari

    c. writ of habeas corpus

    d. writ of continuing mandamus

30. _____ is the failure to act when it is a legal duty to do so. It is also the deliberate act of not narrating details in full, sometimes in favor of one party or to discredit another.

    a. omission

    b. garnishment

    c. restitution

    d. breach of contract

31. Newly certified and appointed corrections officers are required to undergo a _____ period, usually 24 months, to complete the training course that their respective facilities have prescribed. Students who fail the course are likely to be terminated from work.

    a. preliminary

    b. probationary

    c. promotional

    d. prudential

32. Shift assignments make up the correctional officers' _____ .

    a. compensatory damage

    b. restitution procedure

    c. time in grade promotions

    d. work schedule

33. The procedure where accused persons are formally read the charges filed against them, and their opportunity to enter a plea before a court, is called
_____ .

    a. prima facie

    b. detention

    c. due process

    d. arraignment

34. A person who engages in sexual activity with a minor under the age of consent may be held liable for _____ .

    a. statutory rape

    b. non-major offense

    c. oral defamation

    d. child support

35. A person who is convicted of wrongful death must have been involved in the
_____ .

    a. deliberate killing of a middle-school student who was unable to answer the test correctly

    b. premeditated slaughter of an animal, such as a neighbor's pet or a farmer's cattle

    c. commission of an irresponsible action that caused the death of another person

    d. attempt to commit suicide

36. The type of legal writ that orders the recipient to produce tangible pieces of evidence, or other such documents, is called_____ .

    a. court summons

    b. deposition papers

    c. subpoena duces tecum

    d. testate will

37. **Searches relating to law enforcers' questioning and patting down suspicious people in the streets, without the need for any warrants, are called_____ .**

    a. stop and frisk

    b. racial privilege

    c. exigent circumstances

    d. discriminatory tactics

38. **A prisoner who is determined not to commit a disciplinary infraction, misdemeanor, and/or felony at any period during incarceration is eligible for sentence reduction called _____ .**

    a. compassionate release

    b. halfway-house processing

    c. safe-conduct pass

    d. time off for good behavior

39. **A written document that originates from the prosecutor, and which formally accuses a person of having committed a crime, is called a/an _____ .**

    a. claim

    b. indictment

    c. official proceeding

    d. power of attorney

40. **A corrections officer invokes the _____ in the warrant-less seizure of evidence or contraband from an inmate.**

    a. doctrine of necessity

    b. plain-view doctrine

    c. right to remain silent

    d. right against self-incrimination

Grammar

41. A legal maxim holds that justice delayed is justice _____ .

    a. derided

    b. decided

    c. depraved

    d. denied

42. A correctional facility is a _____ setting where incarcerated individuals are taken. It can be a detention center, county jail, or a prison.

    a. reclusive

    b. repulsive

    c. restrictive

    d. retroactive

43. On average, Prison XYZ has a daily population of 1,657 inmates and this _____ to a weekly average of 11,599 inmates.

    a. translates

    b. transmutes

    c. transmogrifies

    d. transgresses

44. It is not a common practice for a facility to allow inmates to leave the _____ to attend funerals or visit ill family members.

    a. premonitions

    b. premises

    c. promises

    d. promontories

45. During escorting duties, the corrections officer will maintain _____ contact with the inmate as much as possible, if not at all times, to see what the latter is doing.

    a. aural

    b. olfactory

    c. tactile

    d. visual

46. It is _____ of all corrections officers to adhere to facility policy, especially on the maintenance of safety and security within the premises.

    a. imperative

    b. impunitive

    c. indicative

    d. intuitive

47. A corrections officer shall possess the skills necessary in evaluating the behavior of all _____ under his or her watch.

    a. inmate's

    b. inmates'

    c. inmates

    d. any of the above

48. What happened at Dorm XYZ last week was a random misfortune. The accident _____ happened to anyone.

    a. could

    b. could at

    c. could of

    d. could have

49. Bullying in prison is a typical condition. However, _____ extent goes beyond the cell walls and bars; corrections officers can also fall victims if they allow themselves to be intimidated and overpowered by others.

    a. It's

    b. Its

    c. Both a and b

    d. None of the above

50. Incarcerated persons should be treated with dignity. _____ human rights must be respected at all times.

    a. Their

    b. They're

    c. Both a and b are correct.

    d. Neither a nor B is correct.

51. Exercising caution at all times is far less cumbersome _____ ending up injured or being accused of hurting others.

    a. than

    b. then

    c. thenceforth

    d. therefrom

52. Today's breakfast at the juvenile center _____ ham and eggs so not many of the young inmates _____ excited to go to the mess hall.

    a. are; are

    b. are; is

    c. is; are

    d. is; is

53. **Yesterday, two corrections officers got hurt while trying to contain a riot that _____ erupted in a housing unit. They _____ minor injuries.**

    a. has; succumbed to

    b. has; supplanted

    c. had; surmised

    d. had; sustained

54. **_____ the facility director selects will be sent to the national event for corrections officers, which _____ scheduled for January next year.**

    a. Whomever; will have been

    b. Whomever; is

    c. Whoever; will have been

    d. Whoever; is

55. **The vocational program _____ classroom work, community service, and paid training. _____ will be administered by local experts who have volunteered their time to support prisoner rehabilitation and reintegration into society.**

    a. entail; They

    b. entailed; These

    c. entails; This

    d. has entail; Those

Reading Comprehension

Read each passage. Choose the answer supported by the sentences in the paragraph.

Passage #1

The use of restraining devices in transporting inmates from the facility to an authorized destination, and back, is approved in accordance with federal and state laws. Restraining devices may include metal and plastic handcuffs, belly chains or their functional equivalent, iron leg cuffs and hobbles. The manner by which inmates are restrained shall, at all times, be documented. The practice of "hog-tying" is not allowed for medical reasons. It is said that this method of restraint can be deadly because it could cause asphyxia, in which a person's breathing is severely interrupted.

56. What best describes the term, *hog-tying*?

   a. Inmates restrained by this method can die of asphyxia.

   b. This is definitely harder to execute than handcuffing inmates.

   c. Corrections officers are not experts in this method of restraint.

   d. All of the choices above apply.

57. Why is hog-tying prohibited?

   a. It is in clear violation of the Universal Declaration of Human Rights.

   b. It is not in any way an effective restraining device, as scientifically proven.

   c. It has medical consequences.

   d. It has agrarian-reform consequences.

58. **Which statement is true about the use of restraining devices for inmates who are being transported to an authorized destination?**

    a. It can only be made if federal and state prosecutors are physically present.

    b. It can only be made in accordance with federal and state laws.

    c. It can only be made if corrections officers are themselves hog-tied.

    d. None of the choices above apply.

59. **Which statement is not true about the use of restraining devices for inmates who are being transported to an authorized destination?**

    a. The manner by which inmates are restrained shall, at all times, be documented.

    b. The manner by which inmates are restrained shall, at designated times of day, be approved in writing at the federal and state levels.

    c. Both a and b apply.

    d. Neither a nor b applies.

60. **In the phrase, "belly chains or their functional equivalent", what other restraining devices are implied in the paragraph?**

    a. cuff links

    b. hula hoops

    c. hog-tying ropes

    d. none of the above

Passage #2

A subpoena is a written order that a court issues. At any point, you may expect to receive one, which relates to your duties. For example, if you are a witness to a felony committed by an inmate against another, you are likely to be summoned to court and testify. You will be narrating under oath what you have seen or heard as the inmate incident transpired. If you are not available to appear in court at the appointed time for a valid reason, the director of your facility can authorize another person to be your agent, who shall act on your behalf. The designated agent will be served or treated in court as you shall have been.

61. **What best describes the legal term, *subpoena*?**

    a. It is a written order that makes a recipient narrate under oath that an agent can be designated on his or her behalf.

    b. It is a written order that summons an individual to do as the court orders.

    c. It is a written order that only correctional officers are authorized to receive.

    d. It is a written order that can only be summoned by corrections officers.

62. **As a corrections officer, you may expect to receive a subpoena related to your duties. Why is this so?**

    a. There is the likelihood of witnessing a felony among inmates.

    b. There is the likelihood of witnessing a felony by the facility director.

    c. There is the likelihood of witnessing a felony by the agent appointed on your behalf.

    d. There is the likelihood of witnessing a felony in court.

63. **If you are not able to appear in court at the appointed time, what will happen?**

    a. You will be served or treated in court as inmates shall have been.

    b. You will be served or treated in court as your agent shall have been.

    c. You will be served or treated in court as the subpoena-issuer shall have been.

    d. None of the choices above apply.

64. **If you witness a felony committed by an inmate against another and you are summoned to court to testify, what should you prepare to make?**

    a. A narration of events starting from the inmate incident and ending in the way the facility director designated an agent to testify on your behalf.

    b. A narration of the subpoena contents about the court issuing an order to make you experience court life as a corrections officer.

    c. A narration of the oath that you will be testifying under.

    d. A narration of what you have seen or heard as the inmate incident transpired.

65. **Under what circumstances can the facility director appoint an agent to act on your behalf and testify about the inmate incident that you yourself have witnessed?**

    a. The court has decided the case without your testimony.

    b. The agent needs a promotion and court appearance is a stepping stone.

    c. There is a valid reason for you not to appear.

    d. All of the choices above apply.

Passage #3

The Automated External Defibrillator (AED) is an electrical device used to stop the heart muscle's fibrillation, or a series of rapid contractions and twitching movements, which may be caused by the lack of pulse and circulation. In correctional facilities, the AED is made available for emergency situations involving inmates, staff, visitors, and other individuals present in the area. Procedures for the use of AED are developed by the facility's medical director. Typically, the facility assembles a special AED response team, and trains all the staff on how to use it and to initiate action whenever there is a need to apply the AED and save a life.

66. **What best describes the medical term, *fibrillation*?**

    a. Correctional facilities are prone to it.

    b. It is caused by rapid contractions and twitching movements.

    c. It may be caused by the lack of pulse and circulation.

d. Inmates are invariably exposed to it.

67. What best describes the AED's function?

    a. It is an electricity-powered apparatus used to stop the pulse.

    b. It is an electromagnetic gadget that stops inmates from escaping.

    c. It is an electrical device that stops the heart muscle's contractions.

    d. All of the choices above apply.

68. In the correctional setting, the AED may be used by trained staff.

    a. True, absolutely.

    b. True, but only if the medical director is present.

    c. False, unless the person who needs it is a staff worker.

    d. False, unless the person who needs it is not an inmate.

69. To whom is the AED made available during emergency situations in the correctional facility?

    a. facility medical director, staff, and AED response team only

    b. inmates, staff, visitors, and others present in the area

    c. any corrections officer who knows how to use it

    d. none of the above

70. The series of rapid contractions and twitching movements of the heart muscle is caused by fibrillation.

    a. True, it is also caused by lack of pulse and circulation.

    b. True, but only if the staff has initiated action for its use.

    c. False, these movements are caused by correctional procedures.

    d. False, these movements in themselves are called fibrillation.

Passage #4

It is a policy of this facility for corrections officers to treat inmates fairly and humanely at all times. They will not subject any inmate to verbal abuse, and can only use language that directs an inmate to behave properly or face corresponding punishment. They will not use physical force on an inmate, unless the latter threatens to escape, to harm others, to instigate disorder, and/or to engage in activities that undermine the safety and security of the facility.

71. What best describes the term, *instigate*?

    a. ward off

    b. dream on

    c. calm down

    d. stir up

72. The word *latter* in the passage refers to _____ .

    a. an inmate

    b. corrections officers

    c. Mormons and other non-Catholics

    d. Muslims only

73. Corrections officers must never use physical force on an inmate under any circumstances.

    a. True, absolutely.

    b. True, unless an inmate instigates due process during his own trial.

    c. False, because use of physical force is permitted in certain situations.

    d. None of the choices above apply.

74. When can corrections officers use physical force?

    a. only when an inmate verbally abuses a corrections officer and, an the process, instigates safety and security within the facility

    b. only when an inmate threatens to escape, to harm others or himself, or to destroy property

    c. every time an inmate gets verbally abused by the staff

    d. whenever an inmate has invoked his right to instigate order

75. Corrections officers are not allowed to subject any inmate to verbal abuse, and can only use language that directs an inmate to behave properly or face corresponding punishment. Which is a correct interpretation of this statement?

    a. They can only use language that directs an inmate to behave properly by facing corresponding punishment.

    b. They can only use language that directs an inmate to behave properly and select a corresponding punishment.

    c. Both a and b are true.

    d. Both a and b are false.

Passage #5

A reading room for children is a typical feature of correctional facilities. This is to accommodate young people who want to engage in library activities while visiting their incarcerated parents. In Prison XYZ, there is a reading room with shelves of books and this supports the state's family literacy campaign. Inmates are encouraged to read stories to the children. From 1 p.m. to 4 p.m. on Saturdays, an inmate reads one story, to be followed by another until the time is up. Facility administrators pre-select the stories and have the volunteering inmates rehearse their narrator-parts before the actual reading. Inmate Jones, a school teacher convicted of molesting his elementary students, wants to join the program because he feels that this will be part of his atonement and healing process. He also says that he can only read to the children right after breakfast. The facility administrators reject his offer.

76. **What is the reason for the facility administrators' rejection of Inmate Jones's offer?**

    a. Facility administrators are 100% sure that Inmate Jones will attack the children.

    b. Inmate Jones's offer is not within the time of the reading schedule.

    c. The children have suspected Inmate Jones's ulterior motive.

    d. Inmates have voted against his offer.

77. **Which statement is true about the reading program in Prison XYZ?**

    a. It supports the statewide family literacy campaign.

    b. Inmate Jones is volunteering for it.

    c. Both a and b are true.

    d. Both a and b are false.

78. **Which statement is false about the reading room in Prison XYZ?**

    a. It is the only one in the state despite the statewide family literacy program.

    b. It is like the reading rooms of other correctional facilities.

    c. It encourages inmates to read to children who are visiting their incarcerated parents.

    d. It has shelves of books for young people to use.

79. **What is a role that volunteer inmates play in connection with Prison XYZ's reading program?**

    a. act as ushers to the visitors who want to listen to corrections officers scheduled to read stories

    b. pre-select the stories for the corrections officers to read

    c. pre-select the stories for the facility administrators to read

    d. rehearse the stories that they are slated to read

80. What event takes place at Prison XYZ every Saturday afternoon?

    a.   an all-inmate cast play

    b.   a dress rehearsal for the Sunday family literacy program

    c.   the pre-selection of stories

    d.   none of the above

Career Skills

There are 20 MCQs across these sub-areas: Communication and Interpersonal Skills, Administrative Skills, Situational Reasoning, and Observational Skills.

Communication and Interpersonal Skills

81. **Why are accurate and clear details important in writing a report?**

    a. Facilities are eligible for local, state, and/or federal recognition, of which write-ups you will be asked to do.

    b. Corrections officers will only be promoted if they can demonstrate the ability to write accurate and clear reports.

    c. Reports will be used as learning aids in teaching the inmates how to write reports with accurate and clear details.

    d. Details will be used in investigating incidents, judging situations, making recommendations, and/or assessing the facility's overall performance.

82. **To convey the facility's vision and mission to inmates, a corrections officer must be able to _____ .**

    a. possess moral authority

    b. demonstrate fluency in Spanish

    c. pass crash courses in psychology and hypnosis

    d. draft academic essays and journal articles that explain methodologies, approaches, and breakthroughs in the American criminal justice system

83. **Why is Officer Paisley recognized by peers as the epitome of courtesy in Facility RST?**

   a. She answers the phone in a polite, friendly tone, and listens intently to the person at the other end of the line.

   b. She addresses inmates with tact and propriety, although she does not forget that she is a person of authority.

   c. She waits until people finish talking before defending her position in a discussion, and explains policy to new staff workers and rules to visitors in a manner that is not condescending and overbearing.

   d. All of the choices above apply.

84. **In a crisis situation involving inmates taking people hostage, corrections officers need to be patient, self-restrained, and keen. Why is this so?**

   a. Patience, self-restraint, and keenness provide a wide opening for snipers and commandos who are tasked to take out the hostage-taking inmates.

   b. Patience is needed in hearing out the demand; self-restraint, in controlling themselves from taking drastic, eventually damaging measures; keenness, especially in finding opportunities to calm the situation down and/or guarantee the safety of hostages.

   c. Either a or b is true.

   d. Neither a nor b is true.

85. **When mediating between two inmates who are in the brink of hurting each other and causing harm to others around them, corrections officers need to be impartial and just, yet firm and alert. Why is this so?**

   a. A mediator taking sides and showing bias will intensify the hostility.

   b. A mediator who lowers his guard could end up getting hurt when inmates manipulate the situation.

   c. Either a or b is true.

   d. Neither a nor b is true.

Administrative Skills

Evaluate the state's inmate records below:

#1: 9566686-F / Scarborough, January Meyers (October 26, 1963)

#2: 7340293-F / Millflower, Edna Karenina (April 29, 1991)

#3: 9947530-M / Hodges, Reginald Wilhelm (March 28, 1976)

#4: 6239402-F / Fucilla, Alessi Roma (February 27, 1989)

#5: 1394931-M / Co, Si (October 31, 1990)

#6: 9965140-F / Asuncion, Joie Beth (August 14, 1984)

#7: 4349093-M / Mantoloking, Morris Ray (May 27, 1964)

#8: 9611453-F / Placino, Genelle Cobaldo (January 3, 1972)

#9: 2340982-F / Rowlands, Charming Grace (April 30, 1991)

#10: 9719880-M / Le Roy-Smarth, Bertrand Guy (September 16, 1984)

86. What is the correct file-number arrangement?

a. 5, 7, 4, 9, 8, 1, 2, 3, 6, 10

b. 5, 4, 3, 9, 10, 7, 6, 8, 1, 2

c. 5, 9, 7, 4, 2, 1, 8, 10, 3, 6

d. 5, 2, 6, 1, 10, 3, 8, 4, 9, 7

87. What is the correct alphabetical arrangement by surname?

a. 1, 9, 8, 7, 2, 10, 3, 4, 6, 5

b. 6, 5, 4, 3, 10, 7, 2, 8, 9, 1

c. 5, 4, 3, 6, 10, 7, 2, 9, 1, 8

d. 10, 9, 8, 7, 6, 1, 2, 3, 4, 5

88. Who is the eldest among the inmates on record?

    a. Scarborough, January Meyers

    b. Le Roy-Smarth, Bertrand Guy

    c. Hodges, Reginald Wilhelm

    d. Asuncion, Joie Beth

89. Who among the following is male?

    a. Scarborough, January Meyers

    b. Placino, Genelle Cobaldo

    c. Fucilla, Alessi Roma

    d. Co, Si

90. Which is the correct alphabetical arrangement of the following names?

    a. Delano-Carob, Luciano; Knauff, Herald; Stanley, Biff; Eckmann, Walton; Rivers, Xavier; McAllister, Hughes; Stanly, Aldrich

    b. Delano-Carob, Luciano; Eckmann, Walton; Knauff, Herald; McAllister, Hughes; Rivers, Xavier; Stanley, Biff; Stanly, Aldrich

    c. Delano-Carob, Luciano; Eckmann, Walton; Knauff, Herald; McAllister, Hughes; Rivers, Xavier; Stanly, Aldrich; Stanley, Biff

    d. Delano-Carob, Luciano; Eckmann, Walton; McAllister, Hughes; Knauff, Herald; Rivers, Xavier; Stanley, Biff; Stanly, Aldrich

Situational Reasoning

91. Arrange Sentences 1-5 into a paragraph to create a logical story. Pick the correct sequence from choices below.

   #1:   Aspirant 456, planning to take the test this October, takes an online review course to refresh on topics like detainee surveillance, crisis intervention, and use of force.

   #2:   In July, the sheriff posts an announcement that the county detention center has expanded, for which new guards are needed. Applicant testing will be conducted at the start of every quarter for the next two years, beginning this year.

   #3:   Aspirant 123 and Aspirant 456 both fail the required in-center training on facility policy, procedures, and operations.

   #4:   After the first announcement, the sheriff issues a press release that all positions have been filled up and has stopped processing applications for new guards.

   #5:   In view of the announcement, Aspirant 123 enrolls in a thirty-week course to prepare for his testing in March.

   a.   2, 1, 5, 3, 4
   b.   5, 2, 4, 3, 1
   c.   1, 5, 2, 4, 3
   d.   2, 4, 5, 1, 3

92. Arrange Sentences 1-5 into a paragraph to create a logical report. Pick the correct sequence from choices below.

#1: During breakfast, Inmate STU and Inmate PQR started heckling each other.

#2: Three corrections officers were dispatched to notify the dead inmate's immediate family.

#3: The injured inmate was brought to the infirmary where he was pronounced dead by the attending physician.

#4: At 12 noon, a riot erupted between Inmate STU's and Inmate PQR's posses. This was due to the heckling that began earlier.

#5: Inmate STU was stabbed in the chest with a knife, by a member of Inmate PQR's posse who had smuggled the weapon out of the kitchen.

a. 4, 1, 5, 2, 3

b. 1, 4, 5, 3, 2

c. 3, 2, 4, 1, 5

d. 1, 3, 5, 4

93. Arrange Sentences 1-5 into a paragraph to create a logical event. Pick the correct sequence from choices below.

#1:   Facility XYZ issues a guideline on handling an inmate escape while being transported. Essentially, it directs the escorting corrections officer to notify the unit concerned immediately, and to provide the details enumerated in the policy. This is a result of a inmate escaping while being transported to an authorized destination, a first-time misfortune for Facility XYZ.

#2:   For lack of policy, Officer V of Facility XYZ chases his ward, Inmate O, without notifying keepers back at the facility; captures him; and uses physical force until Inmate O is knocked unconscious.

#3:   Inmate O is in critical condition at a hospital because of a concussion that has resulted from being struck in the head.

#4:   Vehicle transporting Officer V and Inmate O is involved in a traffic accident that forces the vehicle doors open, and which gives Inmate O an opportunity to escape.

#5:   Facility XYZ processes Inmate O for transport to an authorized destination and assigns Officer V to escort him.

a. 1, 5, 4, 2, 3

b. 2, 1, 3, 4, 5

c. 5, 4, 2, 3, 1

d. 4, 3, 1, 5, 2

94. Arrange Sentences 1-5 into paragraph to create a logical portrayal of how Facility FGH, a woman's correctional institution, develops ideal and fulfilled corrections officers. Pick the correct sequence from choices below.

#1: Eligible workers excitedly apply for a vacation leave and get approval.

#2: Candidates undergo physical examinations.

#3: Probationary corrections officers undergo rigid training on work policy, emergency preparedness, defensive tactics, and other subjects relevant to criminal justice and rehabilitation.

#4: Females who aspire to work in Facility FGH prepare for the certification exam by taking the appropriate course and by answering practice tests. They read about the benefits, including earning credits for vacation leaves.

#5: Guards begin rotating duty at the intake center, visitation area, reading room, kitchen, housing units, administrative building, lobby, and other places within Facility FGH.

a. 1, 2, 4, 5, 3

b. 3, 2, 1, 4, 5

c. 4, 2, 3, 5, 1

d. 5, 4, 3, 1, 2

95. Arrange Sentences 1-5 into a paragraph that is logical enough to justify staff action. Pick the correct sequence from choices below.

#1: Members of the local media arrive to cover the news and interview the facility director.

#2: Persons trapped in the kitchen are extracted and treated by in-house medics.

#3: A gas explosion is heard in the kitchen and a fire spreads to the adjacent rooms.

#4: Based on accounts of two witnesses, four of the inmates on kitchen duty are investigated for arson.

#5: Firefighters declare that the fire has been contained.

a. 2, 3, 5, 1, 4

b. 1, 2, 3, 4, 5

c. 4, 1, 2, 5, 3

d. 3, 5, 2, 1, 4

Observational Skills

The following image is a photo of the San Quentin Prison that was released to the public domain by the California Department of Corrections.

Study the image closely. Within three minutes, pick up as many details as you can without writing it down. Store the information in your memory.

Without going back to the picture, answer the following questions:

96. What best describes the aisle in middle of the room?

    a. Its flooring is made of orange tiles.

    b. It contains mattresses.

    c. It has thin carpeting.

    d. It is filled with tables.

97. What kind of people are seated at the tables?

    a. diners, most of whom look hungry

    b. gamblers playing baccarat

    c. Hispanics, except for one or two Asians

    d. males, some of whom are shirtless

98. What movable structures are placed in the passages?

    a. fabric curtains

    b. plain-looking doors

    c. steel bars

    d. turnstiles

99. How many decks do the bunks have?

    a. 3

    b. 2

    c. 1

    d. 0

100. Apart from the bunks and tables, what other pieces of furniture are in the room?

      a. dumbwaiters

      b. cupboards

      c. benches

      d. armoires

Understanding the Corrections System

There are 50 MCQs in this area to test your knowledge of administration, operations, and other aspects of the American corrections system.

Communication and Interpersonal Skills

101. When corrections officers exhibit derelict behavior at work, what can be expected?

    a. major infractions by inmates

    b. low morale among the staff

    c. eventual breakdown of the facility

    d. all of the above

102. Early today, the union of corrections officers challenged facility administrators for failing to evaluate the repercussions of last week's riot, which was provoked by Offender G. The incident involved a dozen inmates fighting one another, then attacking corrections officers who tried to disperse them. Although no one was permanently disabled, two of these officers suffered broken bones. Another riot erupted yesterday and this was again provoked by Offender G. What could be the union's grounds for holding facility administrators accountable?

    a. Facility administrators turned a blind eye to the recommendation that Offender G be placed in punitive segregation.

    b. The injured corrections officers were not brought to the hospital by colleagues immediately.

    c. Union officers did not receive stipends for convening and arriving at the conclusion that Offender G should be placed in permanent punitive segregation.

    d. None of the choices above apply.

103. Officer Drake, who is training to be a K9 handler, catches four colleagues videotaping another officer's act of cruelty toward a dog. Why does Officer Drake report this matter to the course director, who has expressly stated a policy against animal cruelty?

   a. Four colleagues have not voluntarily submitted to a drug test before filming.

   b. Videotaping unlawful activity during training is prohibited.

   c. Cruelty is unethical and illegal.

   d. All of the choices above apply.

104. Good rapport between corrections officers and inmates can yield optimum results and long-term benefits for all parties concerned, including the institution. Which one is neither an optimum result nor a long-term benefit?

   a. better understanding of staff and inmate issues

   b. stronger interaction in group sessions and vocational classes

   c. decrease in productivity at the duty stations

   d. downtrend in grievance and disciplinary cases

105. It is expressly stated in the employee handbook that the goth and punk cultures have no place in Facility GHI. When a female corrections officer reports for work wearing black lipstick and green-dyed hair, what must her immediate supervisor do?

   a. drag her to the lavatory

   b. sanction her as appropriate

   c. post her picture on the Internet

   d. humiliate her in front of inmates and staff

106. A "man-down" transmitter is a device that corrections officers are required to wear as part of the uniform. Why is tracking them necessary?

a. to monitor any conspiracy or unlawful collaboration with inmates and unscrupulous staff

b. to locate them in crisis situations like when they are assaulted by inmates

c. to determine their predisposition to crime

d. to assess their agility, stamina, and endurance to stress

107. Corrections officers who have died in the line of duty are honored on a specific Web site. Which among these circumstances may administrators choose not to acknowledge and/or commemorate in the online memorial pages?

a. falling from the watchtower

b. getting electrocuted in the laundry room

c. suicide bombing in the administrative offices

d. suffering from a heart attack on the way to a convention

108. Prisoner Sigrid constantly rants to Officer Levi that she has been wrongfully convicted of murdering her boyfriend. She says she has strong evidence that it was her boyfriend's lover, the older woman who lived next door, who had shot him. What advice must Officer Levi give Prisoner Sigrid?

a. appeal the miscarriage of justice

b. get the media to try the jury by publicity

c. seek a wrongful death attorney

d. have Amnesty International advocate her exoneration

109. It is mandatory for corrections officers to train in basic first aid and to update cardiopulmonary resuscitation (CPR) methods. The new national standard is no longer to do rescue-breathing, which can expose the rescuer to the victim's saliva, vomit, and other oral fluids. Physicians and scientists have approved of the protocol of simply giving chest compressions because these will suffice in reviving air exchange and circulation. When Inmate Briggs stopped breathing, Officer Stone responded by alerting the medical team first, then by giving the chest compressions himself as he waited for the responders. Although Inmate Briggs's life was saved, Officer Stone would be challenged by other inmates who filed a complaint against his hesitation to perform rescuer duties to the fullest. They contended that he did not give the expected mouth-to-mouth CPR. What measures should be instituted in relation to this incident?

    a. The facility must educate and train the inmates on proper and updated protocols in administering CPR.

    b. Officer Stone should be cleared.

    c. Everybody should be taught that when saving a life, the victim's personal background is not a matter to contemplate.

    d. All of the above choices apply.

110. Why were four corrections officers on duty in a juvenile detention facility slapped with criminal charges for assaulting an inmate who had spat on a staff nurse?

    a. They harmed the inmate.

    b. They were found guilty of sexually harassing the nurse before the spitting incident.

    c. They did not file a report on the spitting incident.

    d. They did not take the injured inmate to the dispensary immediately.

111. Inmate Thackerer is a Christian writer who is incarcerated for larceny. He has brought a few things with him to sustain his passion while doing time. Which among his possessions will be confiscated to prevent this from being used as a weapon?

a. Bible

b. crayons in the cardboard box

c. legal pad

d. retractable pen

112. Which of the following statements is false about veterans applying as a corrections officer?

a. They are not eligible because they have already served in the uniformed forces.

b. They not eligible because their military orientation is opposite the civilian nature of the corrections career.

c. They are automatically disqualified because they have post-traumatic stress disorder.

d. All of the above are false.

113. Which of the following statements is true about the use of firearms by corrections officers?

a. They must demonstrate proficiency in launching long-range missiles and rocket-propelled grenades.

b. They must possess a valid certification and clearance from the Department of Defense or Department of State.

c. They must pass a background check and a psychological evaluation.

d. All of the above.

114. When Officers Drewy and Shuaib strip-searched a new inmate, they found a dozen packets of heroin in his groin. Why will they be summoned in court in connection with the incident?

a. It is against court-martial rules to strip-search new inmates.

b. They must testify against the inmate for attempting to smuggle prohibited items into the facility.

c. The judge will sign promotion credits as a reward for successfully carrying out a drug-bust operation in the facility.

d. The inmate has charged them of forcing him to commit indecent exposure of his private parts.

115. Kendrick "Bulge" McDonaugh, the state's most notorious gangster, has been found guilty of murdering 26 people as a result of his crime ring's rackets. For his involvement in many counts of extortion, money laundering, drug and human trafficking, and possession of deadly weapons, in what facility is he likely to stay?

a. low-security jail

b. maximum-security prison

c. depends on the grand jury's assessment

d. depends on the occupancy rate of the nearest penitentiary

116. Which of the following statements is not true of typical corrections officers?

a. In many ways, they function like a police officer, teacher, counselor, social worker, and office clerk.

b. Their only job is to report inmate behavior to the immediate superior so workers at the supervisory and managerial levels can take action in preventing riots from breaking out or inmates from escaping.

c. They are not allowed to bring home any keys to the facility.

d. They are entitled to health care and retirement benefits.

117. Inmate W tells you that he has caught Inmate X from his cell block smoking marijuana, and that Inmate X is threatening to hurt him "at lights out tonight". On the other hand, Inmate X tells the same story to your colleague, but reverses the situation and makes himself the victim. You and your colleague find out about each other's experiences with Inmate W and Inmate X, respectively. What is the proper action that you and your colleague should take?

a. document the incidents separately and recommend that either Inmate W or Inmate X be transferred to another housing unit before nighttime

b. arrive at an agreement between you and your colleague as to which inmate is telling the truth, then file a joint report

c. have both Inmate W and Inmate X take a urine test before nighttime and recommend solitary confinement for the lying inmate

d. conduct a straw vote within the cell block to see which inmate is lying and deserves physical restraint

118. As a corrections officer, you are handed a badge that embodies both obligation and privilege. At no time are you allowed to authorize anybody to use your badge, to part with it deliberately during your shift, or to leave it with anybody. How, then, should you treat your badge properly?

a. put it in durable bubble wrap so it will not be tarnished when your colleague needs to use it during an emergency

b. have a craftsman make a duplicate badge for you to wear to work, and tuck the original in a safe place at home

c. wear the original to work, as prescribed, even when it is raining

d. deposit it with the lobby guard before leaving the facility, and claim it on the next working day

119. In both emergency and non-emergency conditions, inmates being transported should be considered an escape risk. As a precautionary measure, corrections officers who are assigned to escort inmates are required to check the latter. What task should corrections officers include in the search routine?

   a. advise facility administrators of searches

   b. check inmates' restraints

   c. maintain distance between inmates

   d. update transport logs

120. There is an earthquake and during an aftershock, your building in Prison OPQ collapses. You make a quick accounting of your colleagues and wards. Although you find the numbers complete, you note that there are people hurt. What is the proper thing for you to do right away?

   a. scream for help in anticipation of a wave of aftershocks

   b. duck under the nearest table to avoid being hurt by falling debris

   c. get your cell phone and call 911

   d. administer first-aid treatments on all injured, including inmates

121. The deployment of incarcerated persons to litter-pickup operations for a county-, region-, statewide environmental campaign is allowed.

   a. True, as long as the prisoners are restrained with belly chains.

   b. False; this is in clear violation of prisoner rights.

   c. Both a and b apply.

   d. Neither a nor b applies.

122. Officer Mills is caught in an argument between two inmates, and responds to the progressively violent situation before the prison riot team's arrival. As soon as he is out of the scene, he falls ill and is taken to the dispensary where the only people there are you and the nurse. As Officer Mills vomits in the bathroom, you hear the nurse tell Officer Mills to go to the hospital. You are alarmed at Officer Mill's worsening condition, and are incredulous at the nurse's advice. What is the first thing that reason dictates you to do?

    a. Contact the facility's emergency team that is trained to handle the situation, then assist Officer Mills as necessary.

    b. Argue with the nurse and tell her that it is her duty to drive the ill Officer Mills to the hospital.

    c. Volunteer to drive Officer Mills to the hospital now as another nurse advises.

    d. Go to the library right away to review protocol on staff emergencies.

123. Newly appointed Officer Kalabar is being tested for his understanding of general intake procedures. He finds among Inmate Hutch's belongings a sharp pure-silver letter opener that the latter says is an heirloom from his grandfather. Officer Kalabar tosses the intricately carved item into a box for proper disposition. What will happen to the valued article?

    a. It will be mailed to the family of Inmate Hutch's victims.

    b. It will be auctioned off, with the proceeds to be halved between Inmate Hutch and the facility.

    c. It will be sent to the state prosecutor as further evidence against Inmate Hutch.

    d. None of the above.

124. Apart from being physically attacked, corrections officers face other forms of bullying by inmates. Which statement correctly relates this?

a. Combat training is also required of corrections officers to ensure that all forms of bullying are tackled.

b. Verbal provocation by inmates is another form of abuse and attempt to overpower corrections officers.

c. Witchcraft is practiced by inmates, especially those who have migrated from Haiti and the neighboring Caribbean islands, so corrections officers must learn counter-magic.

d. None; corrections officers are afforded a blanket protection by law.

125. Private facilities are commercial institutions contracted to provide public-safety and correctional services. What does the law exempt these from?

a. taxes

b. accountability

c. compliance

d. none

126. Which type of written output does a corrections officer routinely prepare?

a. weekly compliance report on facility expenditures

b. inmate roster, housing assignments, work detail

c. emergency health services white paper

d. warden manuals and user guides

127. What can a defendant do in order to remain out of jail while s/he awaits trial?

a. post a bail bond where applicable

b. submit a character reference from the state attorney general

c. apply for witness protection

d. surrender at least 95% of his or her estate to the Justice Department

128. What is a justifiable reason for Officer Robbins to be held liable for obstruction of justice, after responding to a stabbing incident in his cell block?

a. He has disallowed the victim to retaliate.

b. He has disallowed the victim to seek medical treatment immediately.

c. He has allowed the perpetrator to wipe blood off the knife.

d. He has allowed the perpetrator to wipe blood off the gun.

129. If contraband items are those that are not issued by Prison QRS or purchased from the prison commissary, then which of these goods are considered licit?

a. bath soap from the nearby supermarket

b. birthday cake brought in by an inmate's wife

c. pillow cases marked Prison QRS

d. soda from the director's refrigerator

130. You are assigned as a keeper of a powerhouse criminal justice attorney who has been jailed on terrorism charges. He asks that you go lenient on him and excuse him from cleaning the toilet. What is a justifiable reason for you to accommodate his request?

a. He either bribes or terrorizes you and your supervisor.

b. He is showing symptoms of allergic reaction to the chemicals used in cleaning the bathroom.

c. His inmates have voted to do all the dirty work for somebody who has led a charmed life.

d. His educational background and career credentials are sufficient proof that he has no experience in cleaning the toilet.

131. Even corrections officers are mandated to give a person in their custody the Miranda Warning, in case the latter must issue a statement that could lead to self-incrimination. Suppose an inmate from your cell block confides in you about his participation in a gang rape committed months before he was arrested for an unrelated felony. You do not read him his rights before submitting him for further questioning regarding his confession to you. He moves to suppress the statement he has made to you, justifying that you did not give him the Miranda Warning. What is likely to happen to you in court?

a. You will be incriminated for failing to use procedural safeguards that protect the inmate's rights under the Fifth Amendment.

b. You will be slapped with a two-day suspension at most.

c. You will be ostracized by religious members of the community for not seeking their counsel regarding inmate confessions.

d. You will be ordered to narrate his admission as accurately as possible.

132. Officer Roerva is driving home from work when her sedan gets hit by an SUV driven by a male college freshman. Officer Roerva, apparently in a bad mood, disembarks from her car and starts yelling foul words at the young man. She takes out a paddle from the trunk of her car, then smashes the SUV's windshield. As the student pleads with her, he is whacked in the arm for it. The SUV owner ends up with a broken bone and a badly damaged car. With what can he charge the prison guard to win a case?

a. aggravated battery

b. frustrated murder

c. sexual assault

d. temporary insanity

133. As a corrections officer, you are required to be in possession of the keys to your assigned area at all times. Right after lunch, you experience stomach trouble. The pastor, a highly respected community member, arrives as you head for the bathroom to relieve yourself. Despite your explanation, he says that he cannot be made to wait because of a tight schedule. What proper action must you take?

a. Entrust the keys to the pastor who is a revered community member.

b. Take the keys with you whatever happens.

c. Give the keys to the inmate who will be counseled by the pastor.

d. None of the above.

134. It is not uncommon for prisoners to disappear and return after a few days. This is mostly because they are cooperating with the government, turning into state witnesses against higher-level targets, in exchange for their sentences being cut significantly. What is likely to happen when these prisoners come back to their cells?

a. They will be resented for being "rats".

b. They could be provoked by inmates who resent "rats".

c. They might counter-react violently.

d. All are likely to happen.

135. You learn that an inmate's depression is getting worse because he has found out that his mother is sick, with no means to pay for her medical bills. What do you tell him as the proper and best solution to his cause of depression?

a. that you will have a chaplain counsel him about bereavement

b. that you will have him placed in the psychiatric ward immediately

c. that you will have a social worker address the cause of depression

d. that you are absolutely sure about his mother's recuperation, even if this is a lie

136. You are trained to watch out for inmates who are faking an altercation. You know that their motive is to distract you from watching over the others who have plans of committing a serious infraction. When a situation like this breaks out, how should you react initially?

   a. force other inmates to break them up

   b. let the inmates finish their discussion

   c. warn them as you observe

   d. pounce on the inmates involved in an altercation before they start hurting each other

137. Whenever on visiting-area assignments, corrections officers are to ensure that inmates and visitors are treated in a manner that promotes the facility as an institution geared towards the promotion of goodwill. How can corrections officers do this?

   a. Preach in the manner of a good pastor.

   b. Look indifferent and smug.

   c. Engage visitors in a lengthy conversation about the inmates' well-kept secrets.

   d. Be polite and tactful.

138. Officer Annette, of South-East Asian descent, is an amiable prison guard who wins the hearts and minds of most of her charges. She is approached by Inmate Sarifina, of Western African descent, who has been convicted of bribery, falsification of records, and corruption-related acts during her term as governor of a state in the Midwest. She is terminally ill and says that she has included Officer Annette in her will because the prison guard is deserving and in dire need. What is the proper thing for Officer Annette to do?

   a) reward herself with a holiday as soon she accepts the offer

   b) review ethical procedures before taking action

   c) resign from work after thanking Inmate Sarifina

   d) reject the offer outright due to racial issues

139. What is an acceptable disciplinary sanction for an inmate who commits an infraction, such as being caught giving another inmate a tattoo?

a. corporal punishment

b. light punitive action by co-inmates

c. recommendation to forfeit good conduct time

d. removal of beddings and pillows

140. What requirement must be satisfied by furnishing valid documents that pertain to aspiring corrections officers' eligibility for employment in the United States?

a. criminology diploma

b. laissez-passer

c. military background

d. state residence

141. Facility administrators and staff need to review prisoners' case histories so they can separate white-collar criminals from organized-crime syndicates, or plain racketeers from serial rapists. Is this statement true?

a. No; reasons for conviction are not the basis for segregation.

b. No; facility administrators and staff are expressly prohibited by law to review case histories and non-medical records of prisoners.

c. Yes; lifestyle considerations must be factored in to ensure safety, security, and harmony in the buildings.

d. Yes; thorough deliberation on this matter is required of all facility administrators and staff.

142. What are combined security measures to reduce the incidence of drug trafficking in prisons?

   a. X-ray machines, testing kits, barbed wires

   b. threats to forfeit good time, sniffing inmates, federal drug enforcers

   c. proactive guards, sniffing dogs, enhanced security systems

   d. detectors, cell phones, body scanners

143. Officer Val and Officer de Leon conduct a surprise inspection at Cell Block BC because a prisoner innocently talks about scraps of paper scattered about the bed of his bunk mate, a devout Christian. Why do Officer Val and Officer de Leon think that a shakedown in Cell Block BC is necessary?

   a. The prisoner's bunk mate could be hiding contraband in the Bible that has a compartment hollowed out of glued-together pages.

   b. The prisoner blackmails Officer Val and Officer de Leon.

   c. The scraps of paper could contain notes about terrorist plans.

   d. The prisoner is a pathological liar.

144. One night after lights out, Inmate WV suddenly sings at the top of his voice and creates a commotion. Despite warnings, he does not stop; in fact, he starts shaking his body in a dance. What must guards on duty immediately do to contain the situation?

   a. extract him from the housing area

   b. apply physical restraint

   c. tape his mouth

   d. just leave the lights on

145. Officer Udani tells you that she is being sexually harassed by her immediate superior, and that she has solid evidence to support her claim. However, she hesitates to take action because she fears that she will lose her job. What is the right thing for you to do?

a. accompany her to the state prosecutor the following day

b. advise her to file a complaint with the proper office

c. gather all corrections officers in a covert meeting and plan a frame-up against the immediate superior

d. inhibit yourself from the impending case lest you be accused of whistle-blowing

146. Inmates are allowed to file grievances relating to policies and procedures in the facility, inadequate healthcare, or staff negligence. What examples of complaint or question can be filed as a grievance?

a. overheard threat of one inmate to harm another

b. unjust court decisions on their respective cases

c. unsanitary kitchen conditions

d. none of the above

147. You are facing passive resistance from an inmate who holds on to the leg of his bed despite your command for him to go with you for his disciplinary hearing. Although his physical build is heavier than yours, he does not appear to be in the mood for violence. Still, you are required to remove him from his position. What is a non-lethal weapon that you can use?

a. sulfuric acid that you can throw from a distance

b. mild electroshock device that can be struck from yards away

c. machine gun that you are permitted to use

d. megaphone that can also attract the attention of inmates and members of the cell extraction team to help you

148. Which workers are responsible for checking that all prison facilities, including security walls and doors, are resistant to escape attempts, unauthorized access, and vandalism?

a. only staff with engineering backgrounds

b. just the state-approved security systems contractors

c. any appointed inmate

d. all prison guards

149. What is not uncommon in processing applications for corrections officers?

a. background checks

b. creative writing exams

c. oratorical tests

d. racial profiling

150. Prison Director Caprani issues policy on inmate deaths. Operational procedures include reporting, investigation, documentation, and related actions. A provision also states that only authorized facility personnel can notify the immediate family with the official written account that states all facts surrounding the inmate's death. What situation implies that Prison Director Caprani's staff have committed a wrongdoing in regard to the death of an inmate?

a. The chaplain is made to administer rites.

b. Prison Director Caprani calls a meeting with officers on the case.

c. Inmates who discover the dead body are sought for questioning.

d. Inmate's mother learns of her son's death on the Internet, via the social-networking site where she communicates regularly with close friends.

Answer Key

I. General Knowledge

A. Mathematics

1. C	4. A	7. C	10. C	13. C
2. A	5. C	8. D	11. D	14. B
3. B	6. D	9. B	12. B	15. A

B. Terms and Concepts

16. D	21. B	26. B	31. B	36. C
17. A	22. A	27. D	32. D	37. A
18. C	23. D	28. C	33. D	38. D
19. B	24. B	29. C	34. A	39. B
20. C	25. C	30. A	35. C	40. B

C. Grammar

41. D	44. B	47. C	50. B	53. D
42. C	45. D	48. D	51. A	54. B
43. A	46. A	49. B	52. C	55. C

D.   Reading Comprehension

56. A	61. B	66. C	71. D	76. B
57. C	62. A	67. C	72. A	77. C
58. B	63. D	68. A	73. C	78. A
59. A	64. D	69. B	74. B	79. D
60. D	65. C	70. D	75. D	80. D

II.   Career Skills

A.   Communication and Interpersonal Skills

81. D	82. A	83. D	84. B	85. C

B.   Administrative Skills

86. C	87. B	88. A	89. D	90. B

C.   Situational Reasoning

91. A	92. B	93. C	94. C	95. D

D.   Observational Skills

96. D	97. D	98. B	99. A	100. C

III. Understanding the Corrections System

101. D	111. D	121. D	131. D	141. A
102. A	112. D	122. A	132. A	142. C
103. C	113. C	123. D	133. B	143. A
104. C	114. B	124. B	134. D	144. A
105. B	115. B	125. D	135. C	145. B
106. B	116. B	126. B	136. C	146. C
107. C	117. A	127. A	137. D	147. B
108. A	118. C	128. C	138. B	148. D
109. D	119. B	129. C	139. C	149. A
110. A	120. D	130. B	140. D	150. D

References

American Red Cross. (2014). *Adult First Aid/CPR/AED Ready Reference.*

Bureau of Justice Statistics – Office of Justice Programs. (2013). *Recidivism.*

Bureau of Justice Statistics – Office of Justice Programs. (2013). *Reentry trends in the United States.*

Bureau of Justice Statistics – Office of Justice Programs. (2013). *The justice system.*

Bureau of Labor Statistics. (2013). *Occupational employment and wages, May 2013: 33-3012 Correctional officers and jailers.*

Champion, Dean John. (2005). *The American dictionary of criminal justice: Key terms and major court cases* (3rd ed.). Lanham, MD: Roxbury Publishing Company.

Clear, Todd R., Cole, George F., & Reisig, Michael D. *American corrections.* Belmont, CA: Wadsworth, Cengage Learning.

Ebbe, Obi N.I. (Ed.). (2013). *Comparative and international criminal justice systems* (3rd ed.). Boca Raton, FL: Taylor & Francis Group.

Hoover, J. Edgar (Producer). (circa 1950). *Defensive Tactics: Your Personal Weapons of Defense* [Training film]. United States: Department of Justice – Federal Bureau of Investigation.

Federal Bureau of Investigation. (2009). *Offenses known to law enforcement.*

Federal Bureau of Prisons. (2011). *Inmate discipline program.*

Kern, Lauren. (2000, October 12). Job insecurity. *Houston Press News.*

MacKenzie, Doris Layton, & Souryal, Claire. (1994). *Multisite evaluation of shock incarceration.* College Park, MD: University of Maryland – Department of Criminal Justice and Criminology.

Olson, David E., PhD. (2011). *Sheridan Correctional Center Therapeutic Community: Year 6.* Chicago, IL: Illinois Criminal Justice Information Authority.

Schwarz, Jeffrey A., PhD, & Barry, Cynthia, PhD. (2005). A guide to preparing for and responding to prison emergencies. Campbell, CA: Letra.

Stohr, Mary K., & Walsh, Anthony. (2012). *Corrections: The essentials.* Thousand Oaks, CA: SAGE Publications.

The Sentencing Project. (2014). *Fact sheet: Trends in U.S. corrections.* Washington, DC: The Sentencing Project.

United States Code 2000 ed. *Crimes and criminal procedure*, Title 18.

United States Courts. (2013). *Criminal cases.*

United States Courts. (2013). *Parole in the federal prison system.*

Wilson, David B., MacKenzie, Doris Layton., & Mitchell, Fawn Ngo. *Effects of correctional boot camps on offending.*

World Health Organization – Department of Mental Health and Substance Abuse. (2007). Preventing suicide in jails and prisons.

FREE DVD   FREE   FREE DVD

Essential Test Tips DVD from Trivium Test Prep

Dear Customer,

Thank you for purchasing from Trivium Test Prep! We're honored to help you prepare for your Certified Corrections Officer Exam.

To show our appreciation, we're offering a **FREE C**ertified Corrections Officer Exam Essential Test Tips **DVD** by Trivium Test Prep. Our DVD includes 35 test preparation strategies that will make you successful on the Certified Corrections Officer Exam. All we ask is that you email us your feedback and describe your experience with our product. Amazing, awful, or just so-so: we want to hear what you have to say!

To receive your **FREE C**ertified Corrections Officer Exam Essential Test Tips **DVD**, please email us at 5star@triviumtestprep.com. Include "Free 5 Star" in the subject line and the following information in your email:

1. The title of the product you purchased.
2. Your rating from 1 – 5 (with 5 being the best).
3. Your feedback about the product, including how our materials helped you meet your goals and ways in which we can improve our products.
4. Your full name and shipping address so we can send your **FREE C**ertified Corrections Officer Exam Essential Test Tips **DVD**.

If you have any questions or concerns please feel free to contact us directly at 5star@triviumtestprep.com. Thank you!

- Trivium Test Prep Team

* Please note that the free DVD is <u>not included</u> with this book. To receive the free DVD, please follow the instructions above.

Made in the USA
Lexington, KY
30 October 2019